C
BRAN

ALWAYS HIT

ON THE WINGMAN

With an Introduction
by *Glamour's*
CINDI LEIVE

ALWAYS HIT ON THE WINGMAN

. . . and 9 Other Secret Rules for Getting the Love Life You Want

BY JAKE

America's Most Trusted
Dating Columnist

HYPERION NEW YORK

Copyright © 2012 Condé Nast

Library of Congress Cataloging-in-Publication Data

Jake (Glamour's dating columnist)
    Always hit on the wingman : —and 9 other secret rules for
getting the love life you want / by Jake, America's most trusted
dating columnist ; with introduction by Glamour's Cindi Leive.
— 1st ed.
        p. cm.
    ISBN 978-1-4013-2415-5
 1. Dating (Social customs)   2. Man-woman relationships.
3. Single women.   I. Title.
    HQ801.J253 2012
    646.7'7—dc23

                                        2011019105

ISBN: 978-1-4013-2415-5

GLAMOUR is a registered trademark of Advance Magazine
Publishers Inc.
JAKE is a registered trademark of Advance Magazine
Publishers Inc.
Hyperion books are available for special promotions and pre-
miums. For details contact the HarperCollins Special Markets
Department in the New York office at 212-207-7528, fax 212-
207-7222, or e-mail spsales@harpercollins.com.

Book design by Judith Stagnitto Abbate
www.abbatedesign.com
Illustrations by Mary Lynn Blasutta

FIRST EDITION

10 9 8 7 6 5 4 3 2 1

THIS LABEL APPLIES TO TEXT STOCK

We try to produce the most beautiful books possible, and we
are also extremely concerned about the impact of our manu-
facturing process on the forests of the world and the environ-
ment as a whole. Accordingly, we've made sure that all of the
paper we use has been certified as coming from forests that
are managed, to ensure the protection of the people and wild-
life dependent upon them.

For every woman who's ever worn edible lingerie,

Facebook-stalked a guy,

or gone to bed with her phone on (just in case)

and thought: *There's got to be a better way.*

Contents

SECTION ONE
MEETING HIM

SECTION TWO

DATING HIM

Introduction

by Cindi Leive, Editor-in-Chief, Glamour

f you want your car fixed, you ask a mechanic.

If you want to learn Russian, you ask, well, a Russian.

And if you want to understand men? For God's sake, don't ask *me*. You think just because I edit a major women's magazine I have anything figured out? I spent my dating years walking around in the same confused fog as everyone else. Please: Ask a *man*.

Men, after all, are the only ones who really know the answers to such perennial relationship questions as:

- Why don't they call (unless you've clearly signaled that you're completely uninterested, in which case they text immediately and often)?
- Why are there always five of them around just one woman at a party when eighty-two other awesome girls have waxed their legs for just this occasion?
- What's up with Xbox, Ultimate Fighting, ashleymadison .com, the Three Stooges and *Tron: Legacy?*
- Why do they all continue to do that thing with their tongue in your ear even after you're pretty sure you've communicated that it skeeves you out?

• And, most important, what makes them fall completely and utterly for a woman, love her, open up to her, commit to her, hold her hair when she has morning sickness, and adore her for ever and ever?

Men know the answers to these questions. But the problem is they don't, or can't, always communicate them to us . . . and that is why the world needs Jake. Or so the editors of *Glamour* decided more than five decades ago, when, in February 1956, next to an ad for a $2.98 Clifton Hand-Tooled Bag, they introduced Jake Bellamy, a pseudonymous male writer whose job was "to bring a man's point of view into each issue of *Glamour.*" Jake, the editors wrote, was to be imagined as a dashing single guy eating veal piccata in a midtown Manhattan Italian restaurant. (Go with it, this was the fifties.) His job was to explain men to women: not as we want them to be but as they really are. And Jake—who in real life, as you'll learn, was a one-time Princeton basketball star, navy pilot and New York Knicks captain named Bud Palmer—*did* explain men, month after month.

For a generation of women raised before guys and girls talked openly about their feelings, Jake's willingness to do so was an instant hit. The mail started stacking up in *Glamour*'s offices. Reader Nancy Lee Evans suggested that Jake's column "should be printed on handbills and dropped from airplanes in all the 50 states." Marina Kuchar compared his writing to "the poetry of Alexander Pope" (truly!). When some were suspicious ("Are you really male?" wrote reader Leona), Jake's fans jumped in: "Regardless of what your more skeptical readers think, you seem to me to be definitely a man . . . and a nice one," noted N.W. of Michigan in January 1960. "Whatever it is that makes your columns so good, please don't stop!"

To set the record straight: Yes, Jake really was a man. Not the same man all those years, of course (Palmer handed the mantle to a series of other Jakes over the decades), but always a man. I worked as an editorial assistant at *Glamour* in the early nineties, and since attractive male writers were so often in and out of the office visiting their editors, guessing games raged among us cubicle dwellers about which one might be Jake. None, it turned out: One of the unspoken rules of Jake was that he almost never entered the offices; to protect his anonymity, his editor was generally required to meet him elsewhere. (The editor's assistant, who did the expense reports, confided that Jake liked a diner on 47th Street and, from the look of the receipts, usually got a burger.)

To this day, *Glamour* requires anonymity from its Jakes, though a handful of the men who have written the column have, with our blessing, gone public after the fact. ("We're working on a secret handshake and an initiation ordeal, like reading the collected works of Erica Jong," wrote one, Brian Alexander, in 2001.) There are other rules of being Jake as well:

- Jake must be single. He can date, fall in love even, but if he wants to get married? Sorry, Jake. You're fired. The job is to explain why single men do what they do, and Jake, we figure, should be doing it.
- Readers frequently write in asking to date Jake, but this must never, ever happen. (Too complicated, and too meta. Let's save that for *Jake: The Movie*.)
- Jake must like women—*really* like them. The best Jakes, like the one writing this book, have had female friends or

sisters they've truly cared for, and have been driven by a desire to help women get the love lives they so richly deserve.

- And yet Jake must always, always tell it like it is. For that, more than anything else, is what we all want from the men in our lives: honesty, and answers, and openness.

Openness, of course, means something very different today than it did in the 1950s. Back then, Jake wrote about how to be an entertaining dinner date. (Don't show up drunk? Duly noted!) Today he covers everything from online dating to oral sex; the current Jake recently started a firestorm with a frank column about why men like porn. And yet over the years, there have been constants in the way men see, interact with and *need* women. Powerful constants that can help you unlock the secrets to a healthier, happier relationship.

Those constants are at the heart of this book. You're about to learn Jake's Rules: ten of the most life-changing things women should know about dating and relating to men today. Whether you're single, married or, like so many women, somewhere in between, these truths will help you understand how to get what you really want in love.

But don't take it from me. Take it from Jake.

Let's meet this man.

Hi, Ladies.
It's Me, Jake.

Just a guess, but if you're reading this, you're probably interested in men. And you're probably, on occasion, *confused* by men. On behalf of all guys, let me say: We're sorry. Men *are* confusing. How do I know? I once made a living trying to explain them to millions of women. I learned a lot—and what I know, you should too. It's criminal you don't already! But let me explain.

Even before I became Jake almost ten years ago, I always knew who he was. The famous pseudonym masks a guy who writes for *Glamour* every month about how men think. I used to see women reading his column on the subway to work and, before that, in the dorms in college. I even remember seeing my girlfriend read it when I was in high school. What did I think of Jake before I became him? I can recall somewhat jealously imagining him as this worldly, sexy, somewhat jaded guy who seemed to know everything about women. And that is basically who I imagined myself to be years later, as I approached my big 3-0 in the beginning of a new and already very different century. I had a theory back then that there were two kinds of men in the world—the ones who fantasized about falling in love, and the ones who fantasized about the perfect one-night stand. Since I was the former, I figured I was one of the good guys. But now I can tell you that I was the dating woman's basic nightmare.

Notice I didn't say "total nightmare" or "freakishly evil man." Just an average, serial-dating, commitment-phobic kind of nightmare. Just a nightmare the way most men are nightmares. In my case, I had a dating shtick—though I'd never have admitted it at the time. And my shtick went something like this: I'd meet a girl, develop a crush, convince her to date me. We'd go out for cocktails, maybe accompany each other to a party, get a movie night going, find a regular brunch place on Saturdays, figure out what her favorite position was and what mine was, meet the parents, start leaving our stuff at each other's places. . . .

At which point I'd start to get a little restless.

I'd begin to think, *She's giving me early warning signs that she wants us to get more serious, maybe live together, but I'm not desperate to do that, so something must be wrong. She must not be right for me.* And I'd break up with her. Then I'd repeat the whole cycle with a new woman. I was both a player and a romantic—unwilling to make myself vulnerable but disappointed that I couldn't seem to fall in love.

Enter a *Glamour* editor named Jill. On the morning I got her phone call, I was a hungover mess, hunched over an egg-and-cheese in my cubicle at work. Before I could find a pen to write down Jill's name, she was getting down to business, telling me she'd heard about me from some friends, read some of my stuff and thought I might make a good Jake. Did I want to try out for the column?

I wasn't sure if I wanted to. I asked her to let me think about it, and then I hung up and did some research.

Jake, I found out, is a serious institution. The column debuted in 1956 "to bring a man's point of view into each issue of *Glamour*," as the editors put it. The first guy to wear the mantle—and one of a small minority who have since revealed their identities—was Bud Palmer, a former Princeton University basketball star and Renaissance man (he's been credited with helping invent the jump shot, and he later became a Navy pilot and sports announcer). Bud, being a mid-twentieth-century gentleman, devoted most of his columns to instructing "ladies" and "gals" on how to be alluring to men by way of "more imaginative vocabularies, experimental cooking, flaring skirts, enough perfume" and the like. But his columns were sharp, insightful and, underneath all that fifties-era vocab, often timelessly wise. By entreating women to seek adventure, stop worrying so much and *enjoy* dating, Bud-Jake paved the way for subsequent generations of Jakes to have a more equal exchange with women. From the sexual revolution to the fall of hippiedom; from the age of disco to the age of AIDS; from *When Harry Met Sally* . . . to *Sex and the City*, Jake was there. I'd be lying if I said I wasn't a little intimidated by the Jake column's storied past. Plus, I worried that if word leaked out about my true identity, no one would ever sleep with me again. Who wants to see their sexual performance discussed in a column with an audience of 12 million? Ultimately, though, I decided to try out for the gig, which I saw as a flattering opportunity to satisfy what a Jake from the mid-1980s, Laurence Shames, once described as "a tremendous hunger among women to have a man explain his real feelings—because millions of guys either cannot or will not say what's on their minds." I had always agonized over my love life, after all. Why not get paid to do it? I wrote the tryout piece, and I was given the job.

I still remember one of my early conversations with Jill, who became my first editor: "When you're Jake," she said, "you pretty much have to kiss and tell. If you can't get it up one night? You should be happy. You'll have a column to write that month." *Great,* I thought. So now some woman on the sixteenth floor of the Condé Nast building in midtown Manhattan would know when I tried to stuff the oyster into the parking meter. (Sorry. You want to know how men *really* talk, don't you?) But I got what she was saying: Women wanted to know the truth, and the people at this magazine took it as their mission to deliver that truth. I tried to keep that in mind during brainstorming sessions with Jill, a woman with a knack for discussing the most sensitive, sexual details of my life as matter-of-factly as if they were grammar rules or baseball statistics.

Luckily, Jill took my anonymity as seriously as she took the column itself. The editors never leaked my identity, and I didn't say a word either. I had decided not to tell a soul I was Jake. Even now, the only person outside *Glamour* who knows my secret is a woman I'd come to write about as Blossoms—more about *her* soon.

In the beginning, I wrote about what I knew, which was basically the first three months of a relationship . . . especially the sex part. I knew a lot about *those* months. In one column I revealed what men tell their friends about a girl after a date—which is whether or not we slept with her, and not much else. In another I listed the things men fake in bed (the depth of our emotions, that we never get tired, that sex with condoms is just as good). As *Glamour* readers got to know me better and better, they began writing to me, sharing what it was like to be on *their* side of the dating fence. By my second year on the job, I almost felt as though

I was in a relationship with my audience. At this point, my readers had become familiar with my aforementioned dating shtick, and while some women told me they appreciated getting an honest glimpse into the brain of a commitment-phobe like me, plenty of others scolded me for my caddish behavior. I was glad that they cared enough to write, but I shrugged off their criticism. *Just telling it like it is!* I'd say to myself. *You don't like it, you should date women instead!*

I might have gone on like this forever—or at least until I started watching Cialis commercials with more interest—but the year I turned thirty-three, two women came into my life and changed everything. The first was my newest *Glamour* editor, Genevieve, who had a way of calling me on my game that was both unnerving and exciting. "Go deeper!" was her standard note on my columns. And once: "You've never admitted to a woman how confused you really are, have you?" A few months after Genevieve began editing/counseling me, I met a very unusual woman I code-named Orange Blossoms in the Jake column (she wore this insanely intoxicating orange-blossom perfume). I liked her. I mean, I didn't just like her—I was obsessed. I wanted to apply for a job where my sole duty would be to sit across from her and stare at her face all day. Readers of the Jake column saw me fall in love with someone in a way I never had. And then they watched me slip into my old patterns. The deeper I got with Blossoms, the more fixated I got on how awesome it would be to be single again; women on the street began to hypnotize me with their shiny hair or low-cut tops or sheer unknowability. How I longed for my old independence. (Granted, if I was a commitment-phobe, as clichéd as it is, Blossoms was a commitment freak: She would have been fine getting married two weeks after we met, and she had a thing for asking me questions like, "Why did you say 'Good morning' instead of 'Good morning, I love you'?") Feeling trapped, I stalled. I obfuscated. I wrote about my stalling and obfuscating in my Jake columns, and I received what seemed like thousands of e-mails and letters from readers who told me they'd been with too many guys like me, and that I needed to man up already.

Wrote one reader from New York: "Why can't guys see that wanting to be with a woman they love and admire is a gift and an honor rather than a commitment to a lifetime of heartache, pain and arguments? Oh, yeah, you'll get those things too, but hey, at least they'll be with someone you love and who loves you back. Life is short. Are you going to get to your deathbed worrying about all those shiny attractive women who passed you by on the street, or are you going to think about the one that got away? I bet you dollars to doughnuts you will think about the latter."

Whew, did Ms. New York have my number. But did I listen? No. I did what I always did.

I broke up with Blossoms.

People like to say, "Insanity is doing the same thing over and over again and expecting different results." Not true. Insanity is when your meatloaf talks to you and you're convinced that you were abducted by aliens. When you keep doing the same thing and complaining about how it makes you miserable? That's called being a dumbass. And eventually, my readers showed me that.

After I wrote the column about my breakup, I started getting even more mail. A *lot* of mail. My readers wanted to know: Why had I broken up with Blossoms? Why did I break up with everyone? Why was *I* always the one in control, not the women I dated?

And the question that really got me thinking: What on God's green earth was it going to take for me to commit to a woman? After a lot of sleepless nights and some consultation with Genevieve, who I'd started to call my Significant Editor, I wrote a column in which I answered that question as best I could: It was going to take getting outside my comfort zone—not by breaking up with the next woman I fell in love with, but by staying with her long enough to figure out what it was that scared me so much about commitment. Judging by the mail, that was the most popular column I ever wrote.

Meanwhile, readers weren't writing in just to comment on *my* problems. They had plenty of their own, and they needed good advice. The majority who wrote in wanted to know how they could get their boyfriends—many of whom seemed a lot like *me*—to be better, more committed partners.

"I can call him anytime, day or night, and he'll come running for sex," wrote one woman of her so-called boyfriend, "but he keeps me at arm's length emotionally." Another admitted: "I've grown very cynical with each heartache. I no longer believe in happily ever after."

And from another: "Is there any reason I should make an effort to save my relationship if my guy appears to be more interested in playing video games with his pals than being with me?"

What could I say? If I couldn't fix myself, how did they expect me to fix their boyfriends? The best I could do was tell them, as often as possible, that they didn't need to settle. The second most popular column I ever wrote was probably the one in which I told women: "Relationships aren't supposed to suck. You deserve to be loved, to be paid attention to, to gaze across the room, see your boyfriend and think, *God, am I lucky to be with that guy,* and to know he's thinking the same about you." I wanted to be that guy, and the fact that my friends out there in reader-land seemed to believe I had the potential to make a woman happy, in spite of my recent f-up with Blossoms, was about the only solace I had. "One day," wrote a reader from Louisiana, "you will meet a girl who you will not have to explain your weird habits to; she will just look at you and laugh and shake her head and say, 'Whatever!' And she will be confident enough in herself that she won't have to be given an explanation when you need some time to yourself."

I loved that letter, but back in the world where I had a name (and it wasn't Jake), I was going through a pretty rough time, a period in the metaphorical wilderness. It was awful. Since the breakup with Blossoms, food didn't taste right anymore. I literally wandered the streets at night. I would go on dates with terrific women but find myself totally uninterested. Over the next three months, I got more depressed. Sure, I was free to go see a crap Keanu Reeves movie by myself and eat greasy Chinese food afterward without having to call someone and explain why I'd rather be with an egg roll than with her. But the more I thought about it, the more I had to admit that what I really wanted was to snuggle up in bed with Blossoms. (Yeah, "snuggle." I said it. You have a problem with that?) Faced with all the freedom I supposedly craved but didn't actually want, I found myself wondering: *Who's the smart guy now?*

I might still be wandering around dazed and confused today if I hadn't finally run into Blossoms at a real estate open house. I was checking out a "charming 1 BR" (I figured since I was constitutionally unable to be in a serious relationship, I should at least find a nice place to spend the rest of my days alone) when who did I see standing in the bathtub inspecting the showerhead? Yes, Blossoms—wearing the body-huggingest blouse she'd ever worn, I might add. I convinced her to take a walk with me, and I soon realized she wasn't the same person I'd broken up with. "I thought you were responsible for making me happy," she told me, "and responsible for when I wasn't. That wasn't fair." I'd never seen her so strong, and suddenly I wanted nothing more than to be with her, to love her, to make her happy.

Over the next year, Blossoms and I began, tentatively, to get involved again. And I felt myself being seduced like I'd never been before. Blossoms wasn't bewitching me with lingerie, champagne and twenty-nine-ounce home-cooked steaks or any of that crap, but with the confidence she'd gained from having her own life—and her refusal to give that up for me. As I diligently wooed her back, she basically called the shots: first in little ways, like making plans with her girlfriends without checking with me first, or going out dancing whether I liked it or not; then in bigger ways, like announcing she wanted to buy her own place. When she told me this, she didn't say, "If you don't want to move in together, I'm going to buy my own place." She said, "I'm thinking of buying an apartment, and I'd love your help looking." She was doing her own thing without pressuring me, and suddenly I felt free to simply *desire*. It felt good. Before I knew what I was saying, I'd convinced her to hold off on buying something and move in with me.

Whether consciously or not (she claims not, but I'm dubious), Blossoms had tapped into some secret reservoir of power and seduced me into being the man I wanted to be—and would probably have spent the next ten years working up to being without her. She had gotten over her fear of being alone, and because she wasn't afraid anymore, suddenly, neither was I.

That's when it hit me.

All those cute, desirable, frustrated-in-love women out there would never get anywhere trying to change their boyfriends. What they needed to change were their own attitudes. This is what Jake has been trying to tell women for fifty-six years, and it's what I'm saying to you now: *Women, you have no freaking idea how powerful you really are!*

The truth was shockingly clear. While some men (the cheaters, the sexists, the abusers) are, of course, irredeemable and not worth one ounce of any woman's energy, the rest of us average guys mostly jerk you around in relationships *because you let us.* Because you give up the power. And since it's easier for us to be bossy than to make ourselves vulnerable, we just go along with it. But secretly, those of us who want a real, exciting, fulfilling relationship (and that's most men) are dying for you to turn the tables on us.

Because the more you:

- act as independent and unclingy *in* relationships as you do *outside* them and
- love every inch of yourselves, so-called "flaws" and all, and the less you
- sit around feeling miserable and waiting for us to commit to you and
- resent us for being less evolved than you in matters of the heart, then the hotter you are to us.

It's that simple, really. We like confident women. I'm not talking about a woman who's egotistical or trying to prove how hot she is; I'm talking about real confidence. The kind I was now seeing in Blossoms every day.

A few months after she found her secret powerful self who had been there all along—the self who knew what she wanted and actually had fun going after it—I asked her to marry me. She accepted my proposal. I knew this meant saying goodbye to Jake. The editors had always told me the ground rule: Jakes have to retire once they are no longer single. So I wrote my farewell column and dove into my new life—a phase I went on to write about in a glamour.com blog called "I Was Jake (Now I'm Married)." Today I am the happy and amazed dad of a baby daughter—I will call her Li'l Blossoms here. I'm sometimes floored by what a bizarro miracle it is that I ever got to this place: still whipped by my wife and disgustingly in love with my child. Don't get me wrong, marriage is a trip—usually a good trip, occasionally a bad one. But I wouldn't have it any other way.

I actually thought my Jake days were over until recently, when my original editor, Jill, and I met for a catch-up drink at the bar downstairs from her office. We got to talking about my tenure as Jake and all those plaintive, confused letters I used to receive. She told me the latest Jake still gets more letters of the "Why won't he commit?" variety than any other. Apparently, many women continue to believe they have only two options: Give up on a man who, in the words of another book, is "just not that into you," or wait around while your boyfriend acts like a noncommittal loser.

"There's a third way," I told Jill. "But they just can't see it."

"This sounds interesting," she said. "Tell me more!"

And that's when the idea for *Always Hit on the Wingman* was born. We decided I would write a book to help women deal with men who are like I was in those dumbass days of my late twenties and early thirties. I would give women the tools they needed to seize their power in relationships. The power to:

- quit being duped by lame male power moves,
- seduce men on their own terms,
- walk away from the guys they don't actually dig that much, even though they really, *really* want a boyfriend,
- deliver an ultimatum without a man even realizing it (like Blossoms did when she told me she was getting her own place) and, maybe most important,
- quit worrying about how it's all going to work out and remember that this is supposed to be *fun*.

Of course, revolutionizing the way women approach dating and relationships is a big job, and I am only one man. Thankfully, I don't have to do it alone. I am calling upon the collective wisdom of fifty-six years of Jakes to help me get it right. I decided to go back and read every Jake column ever written, and to interview some of the previous Jakes too. Through the decades, after all, these guys have preached the same gospel I'm preaching now: Trust your instincts, be true to yourself while hanging on to a little bit of your inherent mystery, love the body and self you've got and the rest will follow. "This is a damned interesting idea for a book," Bud Palmer told me. "I think young people don't know what to do and could use a little guidance."

This book delivers that guidance. It contains the ten rules that came up over and over in those fifty-six years of Jake columns: ten rules that will help you get in touch with your innate (but too often untapped) ability not only to seduce men sexually but also emotionally—and to keep them seduced for as long as you want to, whether that's until the end of the weekend or 'til death do you part.

Jake's rules are time-tested and timeless, but everything I'm asking you to do makes sense today, for you. This is not a book about dinner-party etiquette and wearing white gloves. It *is*, though, just a little bit classic, and if you follow it, you can be a little bit classic too. You won't need to trick a guy into loving you or pretend to be someone you're not. Because it's your natural awesomeness men are drawn to, not your impersonation of the latest Hollywood super-vixen. You'll get what you want by being more and more yourself.

Having said that, I hope you will trust your instincts even if, on occasion, they diverge from what I'm telling you in this book. I also want you to read on with this last bit of information in mind: Relationships aren't as fragile as you think. If you're with the right person, love is very hard to screw up. So don't worry so much. Blossoms didn't screw it up in the beginning of our relationship when she broke into my e-mail account and read every message from every person whose name she didn't recognize (I forgave her because I knew it was a moment of insanity); and amazingly, I didn't even screw it up when I broke up with her. We are together now because she found her power and because she showed me that it was okay to give up some of mine. Part of the reason I'm writing this book is because I want no less for my own daughter when she starts dating (sometime circa 2075, if I'm lucky). I hope *Always Hit on the Wingman* helps all the women who wrote me letters when I was Jake, the women who are still writing to him now . . . and my little girl in the very distant future.

I hope it helps you, too.

SECTION ONE

MEETING HIM

Wow. You showed up! Thanks for coming. It's truly an honor to have you here, reading this book. And by the way, you look . . . wow. But you're not here to get chatted up by some invisible author. You're here to meet someone *real*. Someone who appreciates just how gorgeous and quirky and smart you are. And yes, that dude *does* exist. (In fact, dozens of him may exist.) And you don't need a black belt in flirting to sweep him off his feet. All you need is to believe in your secret power. That's right, your *secret power*. This section will teach you to find that power and use it to meet the guy you want, the way you want. So without further ado . . .

Always Hit on the Wingman

It's the World's Best—and Most Empowering—Flirting Technique

So, where to start? How about at the very beginning—the moment you lay eyes on a man you like, and want him to lay eyes back on you.

There you are, out for the night, in your dry-clean-only jeans, wearing perfume, looking hot, smelling edible. You've done and redone your hair so it looks the right kind of messy. And you see this guy you wouldn't mind talking to. Say it's a guy you've met once or twice in passing, and thought, *Why isn't* he *at the parties I go to?* But here you are, at a party, and so is he. What's the natural thing to do? Yeah, the natural thing to do is freeze.

Seriously. It's *natural*. Don't feel bad about it. He's probably a little terrified too. So don't let a little case of the nerves stop you from walking across the room and striking up a conversation. How? you ask. Hang on for a little story about the world's best first-few-minutes flirting technique. It's so good that it's actually more of a flirting *philosophy*—one you should keep on using at every stage of your relationship, forever!

The year was 2000. I was with my friend Mark at a house party. The lights were low. The necklines were lower. We were feeling all self-conscious the way men tend to when they roll into a place together. You know what I'm talking about: Two guys walk into a bar or a party like some kind of lady-molesting team. They try to appear laid-back, or at least not desperate, as they awkwardly suck down their drinks, ogle women and don't talk to each other.

These lame and transparent characters are called "wingmen." Some people think the wingman is the second fiddle. Not true. If two single, straight guys are out together, they're both wingmen.

Anyway, Mark was my wingman on this night, and I was his. I came back from the bathroom and saw a gorgeous woman chatting him up. I'd noticed her when she'd walked in, but I had quickly become distracted by another woman at the party whom I'd slept with once—and never called after. Should I do it again and hate myself? Not do it again and hate myself? I was too absorbed in this internal debate to actually put all that aside and approach someone new.

Ms. Gorgeous had blond, almost freakishly long hair. If you were a hair fetishist and you saw her at this party, you'd have had some kind of aneurysm. And there she was, talking to my wingman.

"She's from Delaware," Mark filled me in.

"You don't say," I replied.

"Look at that hair! Wouldn't you think she should be from Sweden or something? Or at least Minnesota?"

Ms. Gorgeous laughed and put a hand on Mark's arm. I still remember the dread I felt when I saw that hand touch his arm. You know a flirty touch when you see one. With that little brush of her long fingers, she became at once more desirable and more unattainable. I figured that since she was after Mark—and I didn't have a chance with her—I would at least try to make her laugh. And I spent the next half hour in that attempt, not wanting to piss off Mark, but curious whether she wanted me to stick around. Eventually, when I went to the bar area to get another drink, Ms. Gorgeous said she'd come with me. *Yes!* I was thinking. *I got her!* Little did I know it was *she* who'd gotten *me*.

Flash forward three months to my bedroom: Ms. Gorgeous and I are a couple and will be for another glorious and tumultuous six months. We are naked in bed, eating take-out sushi and talking about the night we met. She looks at me slyly and says, "You know, I never wanted to talk to Mark in the first place. I was just trying to get to you."

"Shut the f*** up!" I say.

"Are you kidding me that you didn't know that?"

"All these months I thought you were harboring some unresolved attraction to Mark!" I say. "And all this time I've actually felt guilty around Mark, like I stole you from him."

"It's one of the greatest tricks of all time," says Ms. Gorgeous. "Always hit on the wingman."

Always hit on the wingman. It was so simple, so perfectly tailored to men's innate competitiveness, so . . . genius! Ms. Gorgeous was right: The Wingman Technique is probably one of the most effective seduction tactics ever. Not convinced? Here are four reasons it works:

1) Flirting goes best when it feels effortless. Imagine the man of your dreams hanging out at a party near the beer cooler with his friend Mark (work with me, it's an exercise). Now imagine you have to go up and talk to him. How do you feel? Like you're about to go skydiving, only without that little backpack that has the parachute in it? Of course. You're terrified. And damn it, now that you've let the moment pass, he's talking to that chick in the Uggs. Or worse, he's getting bored and making his way to the door.

Now imagine that Mr. Dreamboat Dude isn't there. It's just Mark. Mark in the mock turtleneck, with the bad sideburns. If you were forced to go talk to him, would you be nervous? I didn't think so.

Think about it like a job interview. There's a truism that your best interview is always for the job you don't want. Flirting is the same way. Have you ever noticed how effortlessly cute you are when you're talking to someone you're not attracted to? How you're always getting the wrong guy to eat out of your hand? The best part of the Wingman Technique is that you get to be effortlessly cute and confident and relaxed *in front of the guy you actually like.*

Hitting on the wingman is like interviewing for the job that you don't want, with a recruiter for your dream job standing right there, very impressed.

Big caveat: There's a difference between flirting and coming on like a starved velociraptor. I bet you can guess which side of the fence to stay on. Go easy. Be subtle. If you go overboard, you'll seem desperate—or possibly nuts.

2) Men crave what they don't have. Here's the *second* reason the Wingman Technique works. I call it the Cheeseburger Principle: When a guy sees his friend eating a cheeseburger, he instantly becomes hungry for a cheeseburger. Even if he just ate. Even if he's trying really hard to be a vegetarian. Watching a woman flirt with his friend has the same effect. It makes a guy realize she is . . . no, not a piece of meat, but yummy looking, and worth getting hungry for.

3) Competition makes the heart beat harder. This point is an extension of the Cheeseburger Principle: If men think something— or someone—is too easily attained, we worry we may be too good for it. Just like every other bad habit we have, this one surely goes back to our caveman days, when "getting the girl" meant chasing her other suitor sixteen miles, pushing him down a hill and rendering him unconscious with a good bonk to the head. As exhilarating as it is to get close to a beautiful woman, it's even more of a rush if we have to (figuratively) bonk someone over the head to claim that spot. More centered, together, enlightened dudes may be above this way of thinking, but sadly, most men aren't there yet. So let your crush see you as a challenge to win over. When a guy gets the chance to talk to you, he should feel like it's a big opportunity.

4) You never know, the wingman could actually *be* your man. I'll talk more about this in chapter four, but for now, suffice it to say that sometimes the guy who doesn't knock your socks off the first time you lay eyes on him is the *real* catch.

. . .

Bottom line: This isn't really about the wingman. It's about power. Remember when I said hitting on the wingman is a flirting *philosophy*? Well, here's that whole theory in a nutshell: When you hit on the wingman, *you're* in control of the situation. You're giving yourself a break, making the seduction game a little less intimidating, a little easier. You're being playful, learning how to toy with men in a lighthearted way. (If you don't already know this, we like to be teased a little. As 2010 Jake put it: "There's nothing hotter than a girl with the sharp tongue and wit to lay me low.") And to the reader who says she's not the flirting type because "game-playing" is beneath her, I respectfully disagree. Flirting is entirely defensible. I would explain why, but the guy who wrote the Jake column back in 1976 beat me to the punch by several decades, and he said it better than I could anyway:

> Flirting sometimes brings to mind artificiality and cold calculation—the old clichéd batting of eyelashes, the inviting smile, and feelings that might not be coming straight from the heart. But I think flirting is necessary ... without it we would never know we had reached a point where we were more than friends. It's important to be able to let a man know that. What else has he got to go by but you?
>
> Flirting allows you both to speculate on what your future together might be, without having any strings attached; you

can take chances that are low risk. Your eyes meet, and it is more than communication; it's testing. You're trying each other out to see how many places you can match and connect in.... The game is "What if we both..." and if it turns out to be "Oh, we both nothing," that's too bad, but neither of you loses anything, even face, because it was all in fun; the only money that went down was play money.

—JAKE, NOVEMBER 1976

Which brings me to why I want you to remember these principles for the rest of your life. I want you to remember them even after you know your crush is interested in you—hell, even after you have a kid with your crush! This is hugely important. I wish I could add a line to the marriage vows: Both man and wife promise to keep doing the stuff that made this relationship work at the beginning, forever and ever. Because it's not just important to show a guy your most powerful self during that early, all-I-can-think-about-is-getting-into-your-pants stage of a relationship—it's important for every stage of a relationship, period.

And here's one more thought to remember for later: Even after you've got the guy, keep hitting on the wingman a little. Wait, hear me out. I'm not suggesting you throw yourself at your boyfriend's friends—or allow them to throw themselves at you. No one should be throwing anyone! It's never good to be a heavy-handed flirt, and when you're in a relationship, the kind of extracurricular flirting you get up to should depend on your personality and your man's. If you're a super-reserved type, for example, or if your guy is prone to jealousy, you may want to restrict your minxish behavior to smiling at cute waiters and bantering with the boys at parties. But if the two of you like to live just a tiny bit on the edge, you can take it a little further without doing any damage.

Consider my friend Pete, who's an unusually laid-back guy, maybe a 1.5 on the 1–10 sliding scale of jealousy. Pete's been dating his girlfriend, Alex, for four months. You know what that stage is like—when you're technically a "couple," but you both still act like you're single people going on dates together. Alex is a firecracker. She likes to dress up like it's Halloween even when it's not. You might find her in overalls and a cowboy hat one Friday night, a full-on mechanic's jumpsuit the next. This could be an extremely annoying, attention-hogging trait, but somehow she pulls it off because she seems to be laughing at herself as much as anything. The other thing about her is that she loves to go dancing. And she's a far better dancer than Pete. Then again, a three-legged dog is a better dancer than Pete. Anyway, Alex always dances with the best dancer at the club, and she will practically *grind* with him, whoever he is. The first time I saw this happen, I tried to decide what I would do in Pete's shoes. Interrupt the grindfest? Just walk out and leave her there? But he did neither. Instead, he let Alex's dance-a-thon continue uninterrupted, and at the end of the night, he was all over her. He later admitted he'd been a tiny bit jealous, but he was too busy fantasizing about going home with Alex later to worry about it.

As I warned above: Not all guys are like Pete. Flirt with other men and you run the risk of ruffling feathers. Namely, those of the guy you're flirting with and the guy you're really with or really want to be with. So you've got to be careful. You don't want your boyfriend to go home and start reading through your e-mails. And you don't want to lead on a guy who might not take it well when you turn your attention to your actual six-foot-three, two-hundred-pound boyfriend. This is supposed to be fun, not something you're going to have to call the police about.

So first, know your man. You've got to realize what his tolerance level is. Pete may be a 1.5, but chances are your guy might be more like a 3, a 5 or a 7 on the sliding scale of jealousy. In which case, the dirtiest dancing you might want to do would be taking a slow turn with your brother-in-law at a wedding.

But in general, do keep paying attention to the wingman. The safest flirting is barely flirting at all—it's just interacting with men who aren't your boyfriend. To stay on the safe side, you could always limit it to that. And if *that's* too much for him, my advice is: Get out of the relationship. Super-jealous guys, the 9s and 10s on the sliding scale, are rarely worth your time. In the long run, the restrictions they'll put on your relationship won't make you feel secure, just trapped. Refusing to be treated like property—that's empowering.

Now, if you're reading this book, chances are you're not all settled down and sharing the crossword at the breakfast table. But say you've met the guy you think you'd like to be with for the long haul. Say you're no longer nervous that one of you is going to break up with the other one sometime over the weekend, and you know without asking that the next vacation you go on will be together. Should you *still* flirt with other men? Yes! But now it's subtler. It's more like this: Next time you're at a dinner party with your boyfriend, seat yourself next to someone else (if the hostess hasn't already done it for you). Or have a long, intense conversation with his coworker when you stop by his office. The point is just to mix things up a little, not to do anything that makes him fundamentally question whether you're into him. Just try something that reminds him that you're independent, that you're your own woman.

The other night, Blossoms and I were waiting for a table at a restaurant. I went to the bathroom, and when I came back she was chatting up some guy five years her junior, a guy with slicked-back hair and an expensive suit who clearly thought it was his lucky day. Now, Blossoms knew that I was going to come back and see this, but she played along with the guy anyway, feeling secure that I wouldn't mind. And I didn't. I was never threatened. I understood that she was showing off for me. But it gave the whole night a kind of electric tension. And we were way friskier during dinner (and after!) than we would have been otherwise.

Flirting with another guy can do a lot of different things depending on where you are in your relationship. It shows the man you've been with for a while that he should never take you for granted. It reminds all men why they are into you in the first place. And in those very early days of coupling up, it tells him you are not the thing many men fear most: clingy.

In the long run, provided it's done in the right spirit, flirting and even cultivating male friendships are great ways to inject a lazy relationship with a shot of energy. These are also ways for you to feel sexy and playful in your life apart from your man. The point is to find ways to let the guy you dig see you the way he saw you when he was a stranger you were flirting with too. Think about it the other way around: When is a guy most attractive to you? Is it when you're getting an up-close look at his pores? Or is it when you get to stand back ten feet, watching him wash his car, or wrestle with his nephew, or even talk to a cute friend of yours at a birthday party? That's what I thought. So if you're into someone, give him that little bit of distance to watch *you* from, too. Foster male friendships; flex your independent muscles. Just take a few steps back now and then, and do your thing.

Five Ways You Can Be More Powerfully Attractive to Him in the First Five Minutes

1 **Lock eyes—and smile.** It bears repeating: eye contact, eye contact, eye contact. Hold his gaze, and he'll *feel* it. And when you look happy, the effect is even stronger. This isn't just me talking here! According to researchers at Scotland's University of Aberdeen Face Research Lab (yep, that's what I said), when you smile genuinely and lock eyes with a guy, he finds your face markedly more attractive than if you look at him without smiling.

2 **Compliment him.** Eyes are a safe way to go. Everyone believes secretly that their eyes are nice. It's a bold move, though. If you want to be a bit subtler but still send a clear message, say something good about his laugh.

3 **If you have a wingwoman, be a little touchy with her.** I'm not advocating fake girl-on-girl action. But if you're the kind of girl who's warm and likes to touch, guys will start thinking about you touching *them*.

4 **Admit you don't know something.** Never play dumb, but if the conversation turns to baseball or some new band and you don't know what the heck he's talking

about, ask him to fill you in. It's a powerfully counterintuitive move that shows a guy you're confident. Only the nervous or conceited pretend they know everything.

5 **When you head to the bar, buy *him* a drink.** Taking things into your own hands: a big turn-on.

And a Big P.S.: Ridiculously Hot Men? You Can Get Them Too. Beefcakes, lookers, insanely ripped personal trainers? Don't be intimidated: They are yours for the taking. Why? Because being absurdly male-model hot can give a guy a serious chip on his shoulder. Men want to be taken seriously. Some men want to be taken seriously for their art, some for their power, some for their intellect, and some because they can make a killer risotto with something called fennel pollen. But men who are too good-looking feel that *no one* takes them seriously. They think people look at them and see only a himbo. Deep down, most of these men are not searching for someone as hot as they are so they can go off and have genetically flawless offspring. They want someone who makes them feel *important* and *legitimate*. So if you're a smart woman in the market for some beefcake, try talking to the next model-ish dude you meet as if he's the secretary general of the United Nations. He'll be eating out of your hand in no time.

Know How Sexy You Really Are

Why Men Can't Resist Women Who Love Their Own Bodies

used to date a girl I'll call Laura. She liked to talk about other women's butts—and faces, legs and arms. When we'd go to a party or a bar, she would spend the night giving a running commentary on what other women were wearing and whether it worked or not. That woman had too much cover-up on. This chick's jeans were painfully high-waisted. That girl's short haircut made her face look long. Laura was also the keenest booty critic I've ever seen—definitely more so than any man I've ever met. "She has a pancake butt," she said of one of her own friends whose rear wasn't round. Or she'd see a woman in a club with a big backyard and tight jeans and say, "Someone should have stopped her from leaving the house in those!" Not that she stopped at butt critiques; she also noticed weight, breast size and everything in between. Her favorite expression seemed to be: "She has no business wearing *that*." An important unspoken corollary was: Why is *that* guy going for *that* girl in *those* terrible jeans?

Well, the answer is: because guys don't care which jeans are cool. And we don't put weight or butt-size limits on the women we find attractive. "We'd much rather caress you than assess you," wrote 2001 Jake. We find it irresistible when you're proud of your body, no matter what its shape. The real Laura was a lovable woman—much kinder most of the time than I've made her sound here—and I know she was critical of others only when she felt insecure herself. But one pretty huge thing I learned from being Jake is that plenty of you are more critical of your bodies than Laura could ever be. *Lots* of women have tiny Lauras who live inside their heads, disparaging them. And too many listen to *that* voice instead of the one that says, "You're not perfect, but you're still damned sexy and you know it!" So the first thing you need to do is forget about that tiny critic! No more little voice telling you to keep your sarong on at the beach so everyone doesn't see your little stomach roll and think you're fat. No more little voice chastising you not to smile too much because that one weird tooth is going to show. No more little voice admonishing, "People will think your feet are too big!" when you try on a pair of white flats (yes, Blossoms, I'm talking to you).

If you listened to Laura, you'd be wearing a black turtleneck, your back to the wall in a dim corner with your arms crossed your entire life.

If you listened to Laura, you'd never get laid.

Say this to yourself: "I actually don't care what Laura thinks. I'm not trying to be attractive to Laura." And this most of all: "Men do not think like Laura." In fact, men kind of think the opposite way. They like it when you flaunt, expose or otherwise sexify yourself in your own special way. You know that clingy V-neck shirt you bought six months ago but can never work up the guts to actually wear? It's time to take it out of the closet. I'm not saying to dress in a way you feel cheapens you. I'm simply offering you an invitation to dress, and act, in a way that makes you feel sexy. It's a license to work it.

Did I just say "work it," like the gay best friend in a movie, giving advice to the female lead? Yes, I did. That gay best friend is right: More than any other thing, it's *confidence* that lights you up and draws people to you—when you throw on that light, we want to bask in it too.

So take off that superlong sweater that you think hides your butt! It doesn't. All it really does is tell us that you *want* to hide your butt. And let's get rid of the dresses-over-jeans look too while we're at it (unless that truly is your style, or you're eight, or you're living in Vermont and making organic candles—then it kind of works). Stop going about your life in a sartorial defensive crouch. The first principle of getting dressed shouldn't be hiding, say, your ass. If your ass is big, your ass is big. If you don't want to dress to make it the first thing people notice, okay, but for God's sake, don't try to cloak it into nonexistence. And second, let's say you could hide an ass, and you hid yours, seduced a guy who was anti-booty and brought him home. Are you still going to try to hide the ass? Do you think he won't realize the precise dimensions of your butt—as well as the rest of your body—as soon as business gets under way? And please don't say that you'll just leave the lights off!

What you want to do instead is immediately weed out the worthless putzes—the rare male tiny-Laura sympathizers—who think the size of your butt is a big deal in the first place. Then you need to go out there and find a man who likes a big ass, or who doesn't care about asses either way. Wouldn't it be a relief to know that whoever starts hitting on you is hitting on you *because they know what you look like*—rather than to suspect that it's because they don't? Even if you're convinced you're going to eliminate 90 percent of the men in the room by revealing the true nature of your physical appearance (and believe me, you won't), who has time to date 90 percent of the room anyhow?

Let me say it one more way: The point of getting dressed up and driving to some location where you hope there will be cute, available guys is not to hide from them; the point is to have them see you.

I f you forget everything else in this chapter, remember this: Men like women's bodies. We love women's bodies. We like being reminded that you have a body and that you love it. When you feel the same way about your body that we do—thrilled by the fact that you have it, whatever kind of body it happens to be—you immediately become, according to my highly unscientific calculations, at least 40 percent more attractive.

Even the most sophisticated, sensitive, enlightened man is, at his hairy Cro-Magnon core, a sexual being. And whether he wants to or not, every man is going to react to having his sexual buttons pushed. Sexual buttons aren't necessarily subtle things—they're pushed not only by body parts that look similar to Megan

Fox's or Gisele Bündchen's, they're pushed by body parts in general. So disregard any memory you might have of that old *Seinfeld* episode where Jerry dumps a girl because she has big hands (I believe his term was *man hands*). That was pretty much BS. In my opinion, if a man is feeling antsy or noticing a lack of chemistry or what have you, he may find some flaw in you to justify it—but that flaw isn't the real problem. So show yourselves to us.

The original guy columnist for *Glamour*, Bud Palmer—the first Jake—was a cosmopolitan man who wrote about women in New York City during the fifties and sixties. Understandably, in those days, he never once wrote a column advising women to wear tight jeans—or even the fifties equivalent, tight pedal pushers. But he did have a thing or two to say about the importance of dressing with confidence.

"What impression would you like to give?" Jake wrote in 1957. "Because whatever you transmit will be received, whether you're wearing a body stocking or a muumuu. . . . It's your attitude, not your anatomy, that sets the tone." Now, I'm not totally fluent in 1957-ese, but I think what he's saying is what I've been saying all along too: How you carry yourself—the confidence you feel—is what men see above all else. Wondering what Original Jake would have to say about how women dress and carry themselves *today*? I was too. So I called him. Original Jake is now close to ninety years old, lives in Florida and still has more lady friends than Justin Timberlake. He talks like Jack Lemmon in *The Apartment*—he must have been quite a charmer back in the day (and I'll bet he still is). He told me he thought that women had lost something big

since he was Jake. He said they'd lost sight of what it is they're saying about themselves just by getting dressed and walking out of
the house.

"I used to play a game where I'd, say, walk to lunch in New
York City," he told me. "If I had to walk five blocks, I'd count the
number of women I saw whom I'd like to invite to lunch with me.
There'd be about four or five. Now there aren't as many, because
women don't dress up anymore. They wear these damn sweatsuits.
They don't wear makeup anymore, they don't do their hair—
they've got no style at all."

Original Jake is particularly offended by how women dress on
airplanes. And while it's old-fashioned to expect women to dress
up every time they leave the house, I've got to say, he has a point. Why
do people (men, too!) wear their pajamas when they fly now?
Why do you see people in grocery stores in clothes you wouldn't
want to go to prison in?

I'm not sure Original Jake would agree with me that women
should wear tight jeans and low-cut blouses (which is not *all* I'm
saying, by the way—read the rest of the chapter!), but we're both
essentially saying the same thing: If you project to the world that
you're worth looking at, people will believe you.

Here's the Biggest Secret:
Your "Flaws" Are Actually Your Assets

Of course, you've got to *want* to be looked at. You have to *believe*
you're nice to look at. I don't mean to sound like a Nickelodeon
public service announcement, but I want you to be proud of

CLASSIC JAKE WISDOM

When You're Naked, Just Let Go

" Let's not pretend: The act of being naked with another person is a little weird. It's one of those things, like eating eggs or flying in an airplane, that will completely wig you out if you ponder it too deeply. You're trusting someone enough to bare it all in front of them and then hoping they don't harshly judge your (freckled, dimpled, what-have-you) business.

Here's the thing, though: Being naked with someone is a pact, a sacred oath. The two of you are agreeing to step outside of your inhibitions and insecurities for a while and simply be. Putting caveats on that pact, with no-fly zones he's not allowed to touch or look at, breaks the charm.

That's why every guy I know agrees that the hottest woman is the one who just lets go. "Girls aren't unforgettable because they have 'perfect bodies,'" says my friend Dave. "They're unforgettable because they trusted me—and loved themselves—enough to be totally open."

—JAKE, 2010 "

whatever it is that makes you *you*. Sure, the stereotypes about what men like are partly true. We are obviously not watching the Victoria's Secret Fashion Show out of the goodness of our hearts. But what's also true is that men are as fascinated by your little irregularities and so-called "imperfections" as they are by Adriana Lima's, uh, angel wings. Your individuality is your power. Plus, as 2001 Jake wisely wrote: "Think about it: Your face is the part of you we see the most, so if we're sticking around, it must be fine with us."

Now, take women with "real"-looking bodies (that is, 97 percent of the female population who have curves and bumps and padding where models and movie stars don't): I used to "write" (that is, watch women from behind my open laptop) at a café near a modeling agency where there were plenty of wannabe stars to look at—concave-stomached girls wearing tiny shirts. But I'd already learned the lesson that any man eventually learns when he dates a woman who is runway-"perfect": For about three months, it's freaking *unbelievable*. Then the smoke starts to clear, and he's left dating a person he doesn't even know yet. This is not her fault, it's his—he's been so dazzled by her appearance that he hasn't bothered to look beyond it, and only when the infatuation phase has passed can he assess whether a *real* spark is there. Hence, as I sat writing at that café, I found myself looking past the glamazons to a woman who always came in with her scrappy black mutt. She wore big hoop earrings and had a curvy, soft belly. She got me thinking that those Renaissance painters knew something Hollywood doesn't: Rounded lines just look more inviting, fertile and sexy than hard, straight ones. Inspired by her unconventional beauty, I decided to devote an entire Jake column to the body "flaws" women hate but men love. I waxed poetic about generous tummies, crooked smiles, lopsided breasts and the beauty of women with big, dark eyebrows and thick, lush nether regions. "Sleeping with a fully waxed woman is a bit like sleeping with a store-window mannequin," I wrote. "And I'll take a warm-blooded human any day."

But it was my homage to scars that changed everything for one woman—and made me realize that I was actually doing some good as Jake. Writing about an ex-girlfriend who had a long scar running from her belly button down to her underwear line, I confessed: "There was something about the combination of her femininity and this rough-looking scar that turned me on. It was proof that she'd been through something, that she had hidden reserves of strength." Some time later—and here's the cool part—a friend of Blossoms's told her that she'd read a guy's perspective on scars in *Glamour*, and something in her had shifted.

Blossoms's friend had had some pretty major abdominal surgery when she was eighteen. She told Blossoms that she had a scar that went from her hip, past her navel, up to her ribs. Afterward, as a young woman, embarrassed by her scar, she tried to keep her clothes on as much as possible. She didn't have sex for more than two years. And over time, she became resigned to believing that there was something terrible about her that she should keep from the world as much as possible. After reading my column, though, she had decided to reassess. She asked the guy she'd just started dating what he thought of her scar, and guess what he said? He said he thought it was, and I quote, "badass." He said it was his favorite physical thing about her, because it was just so uniquely her—no one else had anything like it. Well, Blossoms's friend started wearing bikinis again. And if men on the beach checked her out, even lingered on the scar, she no longer felt embarrassed;

she felt proud. And though I hardly knew her, I was proud of her too!

Of course, I'm not the only guy in the world who adores women's imperfections. Far from it. A friend of mine loves the single, errant hair that insists on growing out of his girlfriend's mole, because it makes her more human. And another of my friends finds the fact that one of his girlfriend's eyes is greener than the other to be incredibly beautiful. These are the things that allow us to feel like we really know you. These are the little details that add up to intimacy. So love them as much as we do.

Three Ways to Show Men You Value Your Body

Remember the thing I said earlier about projecting to the world that you're worth looking at? Here's how:

1) At least once, try dressing outside your comfort zone. Allow me to tell you a Halloween story. No, not the kind where someone knocks on the door with his own severed head (though that's a good one). This is about my friend Ann, from college. Ann was a very tall girl with a beautiful face and terrible posture. She was five-foot-ten but slumped so much she ended up being more like five-foot-six. Every time she got up to cross a room, it was as if she were making a silent apology for taking up too much space. It drove me crazy, but it wasn't really my place to say anything. Anyway, Ann was really into this guy we knew—let's call him Richard.

Richard, of course, never noticed her, though she said by far the most trenchant things in our Faulkner seminar.

Then one night I threw a Halloween party at my place. Ann came as Marie Antoinette. She'd made the costume herself. It was this wedding-cake dress, a wig of towering height, and some kind of internal bustier that made her bosom heave in that eighteenth-century kind of way. The first thing she did when she walked in the door was ask me if the getup was too racy. No, I said, it's not too racy; it's just racy enough.

It wasn't just the outfit that was different that night. Ann seemed to feel different in it. She had an attitude like she deserved to be in the room, deserved to be looked at. Maybe it had something to do with playing a queen. And yes, of course, Richard noticed her that night. And yes, of course, she realized Richard was kind of a dolt. But she did go home with a very cool guy who was dressed up as a cheerleader. After that night, I swear to you that Ann started walking differently, dressing differently and apparently feeling differently. She went from being the mousiest girl in the room to, by far, the prettiest. Watching her was kind of like watching a coming-of-age teen movie, but even better.

So why wait for Halloween? Why not try being a sexier, more confident version of yourself *tonight*? Having the guts to be the sexy you is a potent kind of power. Your "costume" might be tighter jeans, or a see-through T-shirt exposing your red bra (please!), or a business suit, or a pair of smarty-pants eyeglasses instead of your usual contacts. It might not even require changing your clothes. Maybe you'll spring for a blowout, or put on heavier eye makeup, or paint your nails dark purple, or walk like a dancer instead of an embarrassed thirteen-year-old girl. Whatever it is you do this one time, just hold on to the feeling it gives you. Believe me, men will pick up on the change in your vibe—and love it.

2) Please don't make us feel bad for liking your body! "Pretty much nothing in our day beats looking at you in the buff," wrote 2009 Jake. I couldn't agree more. And pretty much nothing's worse than when you make us feel like that's a *bad* thing. I remember meeting a girl named Emily when I was in my late twenties. She was infectiously cute, a little chubby at her curvy parts—but I was, and still am, into that. (Side note: Blossoms was, and still is, rail thin. I'm also into *that*.) We were hanging out at my friend Sean's, at an Oscar party, and we spent the whole night talking (and drinking). Then I asked her over to my place for a nightcap. She was very interested in having sex, but she wanted to keep most of her clothes on while we did it, and she kept guiding my hands away from her belly. Now, a little shyness—or even a heaping helping of shyness—is kind of cute. To the right guy, it's hot. But Emily wasn't shy in any other way. Her self-consciousness made her seem angry, pouty, passive. I kept thinking she didn't want to be there, then, with me, which really killed the mood. We'd start making out, I'd put my hands under her shirt and she'd swat them away, almost a little annoyed. I turned on the light to go to the bathroom, and she turned it off immediately and said, "Don't do that!" Men are trying to read all the cues, same as you. And the cue she was giving me was that she was unhappy. Eventually, I told her I was tired. The idea of sex with this woman who seemed to resent me for wanting to take off her clothes seemed like a bad idea. At first I thought she wasn't into it, or me; I came to realize that she wasn't into *herself*—

which I have total compassion for. But it just didn't make any of what we were doing together *fun*. She went home. I fell asleep. We never saw each other again.

Being afraid that someone is going to see the parts of your body you don't like—that's not sexy, that's fraught. And even worse, it's giving up power. If you want to feel powerful in your relationship and, in this case, in the bedroom, you need to feel okay about looking the way you look and find someone who thinks it's fantastic. Otherwise, you'll always feel like you're tricking someone into being attracted to you, and you'll never be comfortable in the bedroom or in your love life that way.

Also, a little tough love here: It's offensive when you essentially tell us not to be attracted to you. As Jake from 1979 put it, "The woman who deems herself unbeautiful makes a decision for me that I would rather make for myself: She has decided what I should find appealing. Not only that, but she also levels a harsh judgment against me: that I don't have the ability and the powers of perception to see her more deeply than, say, the camera's viewfinder."

3) Work it *your way*. This is by no means a call for you to go out and act like a floozy. Working it is different for every person. Like the Original Jake said, you've got to do what you're comfortable with. Just as you shouldn't hide what your true butt looks like, you *should* let your freak flag fly, so when someone responds, it's actually someone who gets off on who you are.

I once dated a woman I'll call Sarah, who, and I'm just going to come out and say it, had really big breasts. Every guy wants to experience giant breasts at least once in his life, because we have thought long and hard for many years (mostly the years between thirteen and eighteen) about what they would feel like, look like—hell, even smell like—up close. So it happens that giant breasts can have a way of eclipsing the person whose breasts they are in the first place. Sarah knew this well. She's actually the one who explained it to me.

Sarah's boobs had been one of her most prominent features since she was about twelve years old. And until just before I met her, she hated them. She felt the same way about them as she had since they first appeared, unbidden, in middle school: ashamed. They'd always seemed like they didn't match her personality. She wanted to tell people she didn't ask for them, that she wasn't that kind of person! She felt like they instantly turned her into a bimbo.

Sarah hated not only her boobs, but any guy she thought liked them. When she saw anyone staring at them, she would roll her eyes. And if she was fooling around with someone who seemed too into them, she'd get pissed off. Then one day her boyfriend—the guy she dated just before lucky me—called her on it. He said, "You know it's really a bummer that I'm not allowed to appreciate your breasts just because they're big. You punish people for even acknowledging that they exist."

Something about what he'd said clicked, Sarah told me. And she decided then and there to love this part of herself that she'd always hated. She would not only accept her breasts but have fun with them—not in a *Playboy* kind of way, but in *her* way.

"I'm done with baggy sweaters," she told me. "There's a middle ground! I call it the tight black shirt." She still didn't like the kinds of guys who leered at her chest. But if she ended up naked, she wasn't going to deny her own appeal. When I was with her, she bared her body with pride, and that made me totally unashamed of my own lust. She simply let me enjoy her. And it was, well, really, really fun—which is, if I may remind you one more time, what men and women are supposed to have together!

I never, in a million years, would have thought I'd be quoting John Mayer, but what the hell: "Your body is a wonderland."

Fourteen Moments When You're Powerfully Irresistible (and Don't Even Know It)

True gorgeousness—as opposed to prettiness, sexiness, cuteness—is a quicksilver substance. It strikes only when some true, hidden part of a woman is revealed (and no, I don't mean her breasts). This is why a $16 million-a-flick actress, perfect and decked out in a barely there gown, may be glamorous, but she isn't necessarily gorgeous. You just can't plan gorgeousness. So when does it happen, you ask? What's really gorgeous? Well, I'll tell you: It's...

... you just after a shower, naked and carefully applying lotion to more parts than you see in a Lever 2000 ad. It's thrilling to watch you revel in that skin of yours.

... you on a business lunch in knee-high boots and a body-hugging suit. It's clear from the body language that you're the complete intellectual equal—make that superior—to your older male colleague. Hot.

... you on the couch, legs tucked underneath you, absorbed in a book. It's a cozy picture, but it's the way you absentmindedly chew on a strand of hair that kills us.

... you, wearing that camisole top, with something sort of sparkly on your cheeks. Our thought bubble reads, "Thank you, thank you, thank you, thank you."

... you devouring a giant hamburger, a little juice running down your chin. Your appetite—with all that it implies—is on full display.

...you, after we've known you for a while and find a picture from when you were eight years old—suddenly, we see your face in a new and heartbreaking way.

...you with a bottle of beer, the glass light in your fingertips. We love to watch the cold brew passing between your parted lips into the darkness of your mouth. I won't go into why that's gorgeous.

...you getting ready to go out—wearing a skirt but only a bra on top, putting on makeup, totally unaware of the fact that we're turning on *Friday Night SmackDown!* to keep ourselves from touching you.

...you when you sing that old Beatles song "Blackbird" while driving. Other songs are fine too. But for me, it's "Blackbird"—simple, melancholy, sweet.

...you playing with your niece, holding her easily on your hip in a way that makes us imagine you as a mother. Of course, this at once gives us a rush and scares the s--t out of us.

...you with your minor wardrobe malfunctions: a twisted bra strap, inside-out underwear (if we are lucky enough to see it). You might be the most beautiful woman in the room, but you're also human.

....you talking to your mother as if she's a friend. There's something about a woman no longer being a child and still loving her mom.

...you as a complete stranger as we watch you emerge from a taxi—first your high-heeled boot, then your long, blue-jeaned leg, then the rest of you. We love the suspense of waiting to see if each part of you will be more beautiful than the last.

...you in tight jogging pants, still sweating from exercise. I can practically feel the heat of your body as you fold in half toward your shoe, stretching.... Okay, that's enough. I need to stop now. Bye.

MEET JAKE | 1980–1984

" Back Then,
Men Were Just
Oblivious. "

This early-eighties Jake took a break from his career as a newspaper editor to be Glamour's resident relationship guru for four years. He covered the dating scene at a time when women were becoming increasingly powerful and confident in the workplace, once writing: "Lying in bed with someone and plotting career dynasties, I've discovered that sharing ambition with her can be a wonderful aphrodisiac." Today, he is an adjunct professor of journalism at a large western university.

How did being Jake change you?
Before writing this column, I was a news guy. I did hard news. I hadn't done a lot of thinking about the modern relationship from the woman's perspective. It was very eye-opening. I never realized how profoundly seriously young women took relationships—how they were looking in the tea leaves and trying to read the

meaning of something a guy had done, which, half the time, given how clueless guys at that time were, didn't mean anything. It made me much more conscious, and it made me take the pain of young women a lot more seriously. I had to think about how seriously *I* took things, and then quadruple that.

What was the most profound thing you learned about men from all that analyzing you did?
How obtuse and insensitive men were. Part of it was the time—back then, men were just oblivious. I mean, the word "relationship" wasn't really even in men's vocabulary at the time. Now, at least as far as I can tell from my students—I teach nonfiction writing now—men are more aware about what women are like, what they expect and how they think.

Do you think the dating landscape has changed much since you were Jake?
Oh, profoundly. Things are much more egalitarian now. Young people are more relaxed and comfortable in their own skin. For men, it's a less macho culture now, despite what beer commercials would have you believe. It's all for the good.

What was the most important thing you ever wrote as Jake?
It was the same message that I'd try to give whenever it was applicable. In every column, if the opportunity arose, I would tell women to take about ten breaths. To step back and realize that men see relationships in a *very* different way. I would tell women not to feel ignored. It's not you, it's just the way his psyche works—he's a little insensitive and immature!

Remember, Love Is Not a Competitive Sport

*How to Stop Comparing Yourself to Your
Friends and Find Your Own "Power Song"*

Before I became Jake, I was a woman-gazer. But writing under the secret cloak of Jake taught me to be a woman-*observer*. Gazing is about taking in the scenery, like, say, a tourist standing on the observation deck at the Grand Canyon. *Observing* is more like being an environmental geologist on an expedition to the Grand Canyon—what's going on here and why, and what can and should be done about it? Not that I'm comparing women to large, arid national landmarks; I'm just saying that I've learned to pay close attention to the way women move through the world—the way you walk into parties (sussing one another out before taking stock of the men); how you act around your friends (if you're tall, you tend to slump your shoulders just the smallest bit when you're standing next to your super-petite friend who makes you feel "big"); and when you're at your funniest, bawdiest best (when you're entertaining a circle of guys). And all this observing is how I've figured out one of the most common ways women squelch their God-given female power: You psych yourselves out! You get intimidated! And often, it's not us men who intimidate you but other women.

Now, I realize that I just spent an entire chapter (Jake's Rule #2: "Know How Sexy You Really Are") hammering it home that you are one smokin' creature and should carry yourself accordingly, and I kind of hate to dwell for much longer on appearances since, as I've said, they matter more to you than they do to most guys. However! It would be pointless to write a chapter about female competition without establishing right up front that most women care—way too much—about what other women look like. And by constantly ranking yourselves against your female "competition"—and finding yourselves lacking—you sap your power instead of stoking it. I'm talking about an old college friend of mine who left behind a budding acting career in Los Angeles to move back home to the middle of Iowa, simply because she thought she'd be the most glamorous woman in town and, therefore, the most desirable. I'm talking about a twenty-nine-year-old acquaintance who posts pictures of herself from ten years ago on her OkCupid profile because "there are so many college women to compete with." And I'm talking about my best work friend, Liz, who came *this*close to a missed love connection when she saw her crush talking to a typically hot girl at a party (more about *that* in a minute). What these women have in common: They judge themselves far more harshly than any guy would. It's a disempowering female instinct, and if you share it, listen up: Comparing yourself to other women is a waste of your time and emotional energy, and it *will* wreak havoc on your love life, as it almost did to Liz.

Liz, who I call my office wife, is about five years younger than me and works a few doors down from my office. She's pretty, but not the kind of pretty you notice at first. Knowing eyes, a sexy half smile that tells you you're not getting away with anything, an intriguing element to the way she carries herself. A little while ago, Liz confided in me that she had a major work crush on Todd. Todd is a young, skinny-jeans-wearing hipster dude with electric-blue eyes. He and Liz had been taking coffee breaks together most afternoons, she told me. They'd also been conducting some low-grade e-mail flirting—mostly sending photographs of Donald Trump to each other with funny captions. (It all started when he sent her an e-mail with the subject heading "Bad hair day," with a photo attached of the Donald engulfed in a major hair monsoon and a caption that read, "Just took this in the mirror with my iPhone.")

Liz was nervous about whether he was into her or not, but it seemed like a no-brainer to me. You don't send four Donald Trump e-mails a day to someone you're not really interested in. So when a bunch of us from work got invites to have birthday drinks with Todd, I counseled Liz to come straight from her after-work dance class, which she says makes her feel "invincible," get him a little drunk and have a little patience. The rest, I told her, would take care of itself.

Not so fast. On the night of Todd's party, I watched Liz walk into the bar, looking almost post-sex glowy with her hair in a messy bun and a spring in her step. Then I watched her smile fade as she noticed Todd, by the bar, talking to a girl from the business development division, Shannon. Shannon is very, very pretty by generic standards: straightened blond hair, shapely tush, a penchant for all things low-cut. But I happen to know that Shannon is not at all Todd's type. Todd likes to wear old Western shirts and play pool in dive bars; Shannon rents a summer house in the Hamptons with a bunch of Wall Street traders and loves golf—not exactly the lifestyle Todd is looking for. I'm not saying that there was no way he'd *sleep* with Shannon on any given night—it's possible a man could find it in his libido to go home with *anyone,* let alone a crazy-hot anyone, if the circumstances were right. But I had seen Todd and Liz together, and there was serious flirt lightning between them. Shannon offered nothing like that.

But this was all lost on poor Liz as she miserably grabbed a beer and tried not to stare. Liz didn't register the lack of chemistry between Shannon and Todd. She didn't register Todd's bored body language (looking around the room, probably for Liz) or Shannon's equally not-hot-for-this-dude body language (checking her phone). Instead, Liz made a quick assessment of Shannon as the type of woman guys prefer to her, put on her coat and started for the door.

"I never think I can compete with girls like Shannon," Liz told me later. "I always figure if you could have someone like *her,* why would you ever go for someone like me?"

And then Todd came up to her. "Where are you going?" he asked. "You were the one person I was looking forward to hanging out with, and since it's my birthday, I'm making you stay!" If Todd wasn't such a confident, assertive guy, Liz would have gone home thinking she'd lost her potential soul mate to Shannon—just another missed connection.

"Shannon was totally hitting on you," Liz said to Todd later—as in, later the next morning, in bed. "You could have gone home with her if you wanted to."

"Shannon?" Todd said. "Shannon's cool. But she's not for me."

Even though I only played a part in connecting Todd and Liz, I get a sense of pride from the fact that they're still together as I write this, two months later. Theirs is a story I'm happy to be able to tell you—a sound argument for *all* women to stop the self-ranking and second-guessing, and trust that if a guy's your Right Guy, he will have eyes only for you.

No, I'm not blowing smoke up your Cosabella undies. This may come as a shock to some of you, but *men aren't as shallow as you think we are!* Most of us don't strive to date the most conventionally hot woman we can find. Sure, we might ogle pictures of bedroom-eyed brunettes or curvy California blondes, but those of us who are worth your while don't expect *you* to look like that. We don't require extraordinary physical beauty in our dates, our girlfriends, our wives. This is partly because we know we have no right to make that kind of demand, especially given how long it's been since we went to the gym. And it's partly because—as I hope the last chapter made clear—men's beauty standards are far more forgiving than yours.

So, one more time: *Women, stop psyching yourselves out!* If you think you might be the perfect match for the man you're interested in, forget about the competition and find out if you're right. At the risk of sounding like your high school guidance counselor, the best way not to get into Harvard is not to apply. Whatever the potential roadblock is—whether you've decided this guy is way too amazing not to have a girlfriend, or is only into blondes, or is possibly the prince of a small nation in the Alps and has to marry one of his cousins—don't let it bother you. Because, frankly, *you don't know*. You don't know if he's into you until you give him the chance to show you. And what Liz wasn't realizing is that she was already being assertive, already using her powers. She got her flirt out there in the best, least BS-y way possible: She got to know Todd, she became friends with him, she let him flirt back. And then she did what women everywhere do—she nearly talked herself out of a good thing.

If he's not into you, fine. But the idea of *you* deciding you're not good-looking enough for a guy because there are other, supposedly better-looking women in the room, or in the vicinity, or in your mind's eye—that's just ridiculous. And this isn't just about looks, either. Women take themselves out of the running for all kinds of reasons. *She's funnier than me. She's more successful.* In Liz's case, *She's more outgoing.* Stop comparing yourself to other people. Stop it. The important thing here isn't seeing other people more clearly, but seeing yourself.

Are You a Second Glancer?

Shannon—the woman Liz thought she couldn't compete with—is attractive and well put together, but more than that, she's really outgoing. She's the type of woman who loves flirting, sees it as a sport and isn't afraid to call attention to herself. She's fantastic, but there are plenty of men who are looking for a different kind of woman—a more Liz-like woman. Jake from 2001 called her a "Second Glancer." See if she sounds like you.

A Second Glancer, as 2001 Jake explained it, isn't the first woman you notice in a room. An SG is the kind of woman who becomes more beautiful the more you look at her and the more you get to know her. In his words, "The Second Glancer is one of those low-key women who might seem plain Jane at first sight, but give them a second look and you can't tear your eyes away (and we men always look *at least* twice). They're not overly dolled-up and they're not clamoring for attention. What makes Second Glancers glance-worthy is their low-key confidence. Experience has taught us (at least the more enlightened among us) that the gal desperate to be noticed is most likely harboring a bundle of hang-ups. That doesn't exactly translate into a potentially great relationship (or great sex)."

Well said, my Jake brother. And might I add that another reason many guys like Second Glancers is purely selfish. A man wants to think the woman he chooses belongs to him in some way, and it's hard to see someone as your soul mate if she's apparently *everyone's* soul mate. Better to believe she was custom designed for you in particular. And that's just what a Second Glancer seems to be.

When I ask Todd what he loves most about Liz, he rattles on for a while: It's her quiet confidence, her "I don't care what anyone thinks of me" vibe, the way she seems to whisper "notice me" rather than scream "ogle me." Wondering how *you* assert that kind of quiet power? Just by being yourself and by doing the things that make you *you*.

That's what made my friend Will fall for *his* Second Glancer. And he was an unlikely candidate: For most of the last decade, Will dated the same woman. Not literally the same woman—there's been Nicole, Amely, Alexandra, Sara, Julie, even a Freddie. But they were all twenty-five-ish, tall, beautiful. And he seemed to break up with one of them every six months, only to start dating another one a few weeks later. Will, it should go without saying, is good-looking, absurdly charming and fun, and he's really into sailing. That's his thing. In fact, for a while, it seemed like the one lasting relationship he would have in his life would be with a forty-two-foot Hinckley, if he could ever afford it, not with a woman. For fun (and extra cash) he started crewing on a boat on the weekends last year and got teamed up with, yes, a woman who was about thirty, in shape and cute—but not in the jaw-dropping way Will would usually go for. They got to know each other over time and eventually had dinner one night to talk about ropes or jibs or whatever you talk about when you're hot for sailing. They started eating together after every time they crewed the boat, ended up making out one night and then, next thing you know, they were living together.

"I never thought I could be attracted to someone I started off liking just as a friend," he told me. "Now I know that if I *like* a woman before I decide I want to sleep with her . . . that's the real deal."

Will has finally grown up and learned for himself what 1979 Jake meant when he wrote these super-enlightened words: "I can't be dazzled, I can't be bowled over, I can't be stunned by the woman who tries to be a knockout. But burn with the steady flame of unselfconscious beauty, let me observe the way you do the things you do that make *you* feel most yourself, and I'm knocked out, I'm on the floor, I'm yours."

Man, I love a good seventies Jake: Platform shoes, halter tops and hot pants be damned! His perfect girl was natural, unvarnished and unpretentious—a lot like the Dream Woman of almost every guy I know today.

Find Your Song and Things Will Fall into Place

What does it really take, you might be wondering, to make men see your inner beauty and feel that all-powerful spark?

Though every man is different, I can tell you that we care about the whole package: inside, outside, body, brain, all that stuff you can't put your finger on but can feel in a woman's presence. The best way I can explain it is with my Power Song theory, which, thankfully, has nothing to do with either Celine Dion or Lady Gaga. Every woman carries with her a specific and impossible-to-replicate song. (Really, don't make fun of me for this—it sounds touchy-feely, but I believe it.) A woman's Power Song is the vibe she gives off: cozy and snuggly, or mysterious and distant, or hilarious and whip-smart. It's the light behind her eyes, and how her hair smells, and what makes her smile, and the inflections of her speech, and all the rest of the countless things that make up the way a person is perceived in the world. You have your own music—the key is being able to get a man to hear that music. And that, of course, starts with hearing it yourself.

Maybe I need to explain a little more. The song you're singing just by *being*—that's the song I'm talking about. It's who you are, not who you think you should be. It's a way of seeing yourself that's beautiful. Rather than thinking, *I'm shy and have a weird laugh and I wish I had different knees,* your power song says, *I'm kind and patient and laugh in a genuine way that's infectious.* When a man really falls in love with you, he's going to fall in love with the real you, the whole summed-up vibe of you. If you can understand what's so hot about that summed-up vibe of you, you're going to feel a whole lot more confident going out into the world, and it'll make it easier for men to hear that as well. Liking your own music is a good way to keep yourself in the race, a good way to keep from comparing yourself to anyone else, since, by nature, they're singing a different song. You can think of it as a little pep talk you give yourself, or just a certain joy you bring to walking around in the world as *you,* as long as it connects you to some self-love. Too many people take themselves out of the love game before knowing what their Power Song even sounds like. Why? Because they're afraid of being turned down. What I'm about to say is a tall order (believe me, I tried to tell myself this for years when I was single with only intermittent success), but here goes: Don't be hurt by rejection. So you're not right for someone. So what? Maybe he's an A-hole. Maybe he's not ready. Maybe he's not attracted to you. Are *you* attracted to every single person you meet? The next time you're terrified to approach That Guy, just remember the last nice guy you rejected. You were flattered by his attention, right? That's the worst thing that could happen if this doesn't work out—you flatter someone.

Stop Racing Your Friends to the Finish Line

What's that? Oh, sorry, I couldn't hear you over my Power Song. But let me dial it down and get back, now, to the core message of Jake's Rule #3: It's your love life, so live it on *your* terms. Nobody else's. I have an ex—we'll call her Cleo—who was constantly gauging where she was in life compared to her friends, her enemies, women she barely knew. "Everyone's engaged but me," she used to say to people. "Sue's having a baby, and I'm still on the Pill." She'd talk about how a woman she worked with had the most devoted boyfriend in the world, or the most romantic, or at least a guy with a vacation house. It was awful for me because it made me feel guilty. I thought all the time that maybe I was holding her back in her life, that I was an inferior boyfriend, that I was the reason she was in last place. I was the reason she was *abnormal*. It made the entire question of our future feel very dark, and it filled me with a sense of dread. It also made me resentful. I don't want to get married to keep up with someone's friends! I don't want to have a baby because Sue had a baby! The whole thing made my life miserable for the last few months of our relationship.

But as miserable as Cleo's compare-a-thon made me, it made her life even worse. She walked around feeling like a failure, like there was something wrong with her and everyone could see it. It got even more pronounced after we broke up (she's the one who finally ended it; I have a lot of shame about that). That was the song she was singing with her presence in the world: *I'm a failure and unworthy, and I'm ashamed and resentful because of it.* Not exactly a power ballad.

So what song are *you* singing? I can guarantee you'll find it—and that men will fall for it—a lot faster if you're too busy loving life to think about how you rank with anyone but yourself.

That's the woman we *all* want to be with—not the thin, big-busted girl who'll put out, or whatever the intimidating cliché in your head may be. That's the woman men find irresistible. That's the woman with power.

Male "Turn-ons" That Aren't

So many women I heard from as Jake wanted to know what men really thought of how they acted on dates—and what they should do more of, or less of. Well, I'm here to relieve you of some stress. These three seduction moves don't really work, so you might as well drop 'em.

When you laugh at everything we say

We think we're pretty funny. But we know we're not *that* funny. So you don't have to pretend. If you laugh—instead of cutely rolling your eyes—even when we make that lame joke about the "catch of the day" on the menu being right across from us? We'll think maybe you're a little bonkers.

Jake of 1977 put it like this: "I would rather make a woman laugh than anything else we could do in public. Her laugh tells me I've surprised her by knowing something she thought only she knew. It's the beginning of intimacy. . . . So the laugh should *never be faked*." Okay, I italicized his words. He didn't. But I'm sure he meant to.

When you talk about other guys

I know there are a lot of people and books and Web sites that tell you this is a great turn-on—it makes you appear to be sought after! But in reality, we don't want to talk about what a jerk-wad your ex was. It makes you seem bitter, and makes us wonder what you'd say about us if things didn't work out.

When you dress like a socialite

No matter how sexy and beautiful you look in something extremely high-maintenance, we still see the really expensive vase our mother told us not to play with because we might break it. Bottom line: Fancy clothes just don't impress us like they impress you. (If you want a clue to how little we know about fancy clothes, wait until we buy you a dress for your birthday. In advance: Sorry!)

SECTION TWO

DATING HIM

So you've found someone you're interested in dating. Maybe you're *very* interested. But there are some hitches. (This is life, after all. There always are.) Maybe you still can't figure out how he feels about you. Or how you feel about *him*. Or where the whole thing's going. But still, you're wondering: Is he a keeper? And if so, how do you actually, you know, keep him? Here's how: You're going to seduce him, mind, body and heart. No, not with lingerie. Not with sex. But by using your secret powers. Ready? Turn the page.

Repeat After Me: The Best Men Don't Send Expensive Flowers

Why You Shouldn't Be Blinded by Clichéd Acts of Chivalry, and How to Spot a True Knight

f you don't like this chapter's rule—and I think it's going to be the most controversial one in the book—you should blame my mom.

Now, I don't want to be reductive here; there is no shortage of things that influence us as we grow up, like genetics, or whether you were breast-fed, or if you were beaten up in third grade by a kid named Kevin (not that I know anything about that). But if I had only an elevator ride's time to sum up my dynamic with women,

I would explain this: I was raised in the Midwest by a strong-minded mother who'd grown up with a domineering father, but had managed to come into her own in a big, bold way. My mother rode a motorcycle, smoked Camels in college, paid her own way through graduate school and wrote her thesis about the patriarchy. And I would say that I have always found these details about her to be incredibly cool.

I learned a lot of things from my mom: how to listen; how to be compassionate; how to think independently. It's probably a little late in this book to be dedicating it to her, but she's responsible for my being a person who is both curious to know how women think and aware of the fact that women would like to be let in on how *men* think. Without my mom, I'd never have been Jake!

So what else, you might be wondering, did my Superwoman mom teach me? Here's a biggie: *Chivalry is overrated.*

Mama Jake grew up in a close-knit, country-clubby society where everyone was taught impeccable manners, but half the men, she said, turned out to be guys you wouldn't want to date, who never had the first clue about women, who often didn't even like women or were actually *afraid* of them.

Now, my mom never said the exact words, "The best guys don't send expensive flowers." But I do remember her telling my sister and me that the best friends and lovers are not the ones who sweep you off your feet from the get-go. In fact, while it may be thrilling, for a time, to be dazzled and wooed, it can be infinitely more romantic just to stand, feet on the ground, and stare into someone's eyes. And it's hard to do that when one of you is way up high on a pedestal. Sometimes, Mom said, being charming is just a 1924 way to avoid being real. And that's just it: Chivalry (the bad kind—

I'll get to the good kind later) isn't about reality at all. It's about fantasy. In particular, the Knight in Shining Armor fantasy. Many women love this fantasy, which is why it's easy for men to manipulate them with it. Women are always telling me that men are easy to trick—wear a low-cut blouse and they won't notice anything else. But women are pretty easy to trick too: be nice to your dad, buy you (and, better yet, your mom) expensive flowers, refill your drink and we're pretty much in. But if you can't see the real man behind the gallant dude who just filled your arms with Casablanca lilies, you could be in for a rude awakening.

Okay, okay, before I take this rant any further I should make something clear: Being polite is good. It certainly doesn't, in and of itself, make a guy bad. And certain men were raised to be exceedingly polite: dudes from the deepest Deep South, men who were born before 1960, fellows who were raised by very strict mothers who taught them to address all women as "ma'am," and anyone who takes the idea of a seersucker suit deadly seriously. These are just guys who were socialized (as my mom would say!) to behave a certain way. All I'm saying is you shouldn't be blinded by that behavior—and there *are* certain men out there who *want* you to be blinded by it.

In my exhaustive studies, I've broken the latter group into three distinct fake-chivalrous types:

Chivalrous Type #1: The Show-Off

I've met the kind of guy my mother was always warning my sister about (and warning me about becoming). Let's call him P. P is not a good guy. In fact, he's one of the few guys I've ever known whom I wouldn't want *anyone's* sister to date. And he's also one of the most polite people I've ever encountered. How are both of these things possible? I'm glad you asked.

I first encountered P years ago, when the two of us worked together. He's the kind of chivalrous guy I call the Show-off. When you meet him, you say things like "Wow, they don't make them like *that* anymore. He's the perfect guy. He should date my sister." Why? He's successful, well-dressed, well-read, soft-spoken. The man wears cologne—not Old Spice aftershave but a subtle European fragrance, as if it is a courteous gesture to the world for him to mask any impolite odor. Polite doesn't even come close to describing this guy. He looks for old ladies to hold the door for; he will wait for every man, woman, child, animal and dust mite to enter the elevator before he does; he stands when a woman gets up from the table and stands again when she sits down; he doesn't have a cold but carries an expensive hanky just in case he should come across a woman in tears; he lives to hail taxis for helpless dames.

I don't know what movie P copped all these tricks from, but I bet it's black and white and there's someone named Cary Grant in it. If he seems like a throwback, that's because he *is* a throwback. It turns out this is the kind of guy who's been driving Jake crazy for the past fifty-six years (literally!). As 1967 Jake put it in one withering column, "This is not an actual man, it's a counterfeit. You can tell because he walks around all day long with his capital letters showing. 'I am the Good Guy,' he tells you with every move he makes. . . . 'How I appear is what matters.'" (Check out page 65 for 1967 Jake's entire rant against chivalrous dudes—it's eerily similar to mine!) Men who seduce women with that Good Guy charm are nothing new—but women continue to fall, and fall hard, for types like P.

I got to know the dark side of P when my friend Lily began dating him. She first met him at a dinner party we both attended. She couldn't help but notice him as he stood from his seat when she got up to use the ladies' room. And from that very moment, she swooned. Initially, things seemed to go well between them. She loved the way he proffered his coat at the first sign of a chill in the air, and that, instead of going to bed in ugly boxers, he wore real pajamas for her, just like good old Cary Grant. She even loved it when he pulled the blatantly sexist move of ordering dinner for her at a restaurant. (She said it made her feel "like I was his rare, important guest—okay, kind of like a princess.") I think Lily fell for P simply because she was so sick of men who let the door slam on her or never even reached for their wallets at the end of dinner. And let me say: This chapter is no argument for being *that* jerk either. In fact, it's the preponderance of those jerks that makes guys like P so attractive. But as far as Lily goes, she'd always prided herself on being a strong, independent woman. It wasn't until she met P that she realized she also loved being taken care of.

And guess what? It's that deep-rooted female desire to be taken care of—which so many women feel just a little, somewhere—that men like P exploit in order to get what *they* want. To illustrate, let's get back to Lily. As she got to know P, she discovered a different person from the man she'd met at dinner that night. The flip side to his chivalry, as it turned out, was that he liked her to be helpless and grateful. He liked to see her in the pretty clothes he'd buy for her, but he wouldn't really listen when she wanted to talk about her family. He loved carrying her suitcase but resented when she got a raise that put her in a higher income bracket than him. When she gave him that news, he smiled coldly and said flatly, "Congratulations." When she suggested they celebrate, he said he had a headache. When he consented to go out, and the bill for the Champagne arrived at the end of the night, and she tried to insist on paying for it, he got angry: "You got a raise, but it's not like I'm in the poorhouse, for Christ's sake," he snapped, grabbing the bill from her. That should have been a clue.

Later, when she actually was noticing clues—because she didn't for a while—she confronted him. She said she wondered whether his overwhelming politeness was just a way of not having to really get to know her. He was reflexively polite in the same way toward all people—and it had long since stopped making her feel special. He responded by smashing a bottle of her perfume, then stomping out of her house. That's when Lily realized, she said, that his chivalry was just a way of hiding parts of himself. It was a way of treating women like little girls who could easily be bought with a gift or a generic gesture, but who were not his equals.

Six months after they met, Lily broke up with P. She had begun to feel manipulated, and like he actually *resented* her instead of worshipping her. She told him as much when she broke up with him—she felt it was information he should have—and he responded, poetically, by calling her a child. Then he threw her things out of his window. To this day she's embarrassed to have dated him.

P is an extreme case. If you're lucky, you'll never meet anyone remotely like him. But he's the perfect illustration of a point I can't make strongly enough: Some chivalry isn't about you, it's about *him*. And that's the chivalry that you should be very, very wary of. If he's perfectly mannered and great on paper, but you still don't feel he actually *likes* you, run.

Chivalrous Type #2: The Woman Collector

The Woman Collector is a man who simply wants to be adored by as many women as possible. He does it by believing he knows what every woman's fantasy is—specifically, in this case, to finally find a guy who has manners—and then getting as many women as possible to believe he's this fantasy man. This is a guy who, on the face of things, often seems courteous and mild-mannered and apt to call you "ma'am" (Tiger Woods, y'all?). Sometimes, besides being polite in the traditional sense, he is emotionally chivalrous. He seems to truly listen to what you have to say. He seems to feel your pain (Bill Clinton, y'all!). He seems to intuit that you are especially proud of your long hair, or self-conscious about your thighs—and he will say just the right thing about both.

The problem is that he is addicted to playing this role, and he wants to play it with almost everyone. The Woman Collector is typically not as cruel as the Show-Off, but he is almost as danger-ous. He wants to look deep into the eyes of as many women as possible and see his own handsome reflection. So he will be chiv-alrous, but he will often be chivalrous while he's lying to you about not dating other people. And he's apt to leave a trail of women behind him who believe they are incredibly special to him, who think they have a connection to him no one else could have. With a man like this, you never get more than a tiny, tiny slice. Which, for an amazing woman like you, should not be enough. Part of your power comes from knowing that you deserve much, much more.

Chivalrous Type #3: The Pedestal Guy

Some men are chivalrous not because they're megalomaniacs but because they're just the opposite. They get off on being whipped. Strange but true, so hear me out. My friend Marie dated a man named Arman. They'd met once on the street, and he'd become obsessed. He called to ask her out, and when she said she couldn't go to dinner because she was sick, he showed up at her apartment with chicken soup. Any other time, that would have creeped her out a little, but at this moment she appreciated the over-the-top gesture. "I'd just been dumped by a guy who was a total insensitive jerk," she told me. "So this felt like a relief."

Arman was the consummate gentleman. When he went to London on business, he brought her back a cashmere scarf and dropped it off in a box for her at her office. He picked up her dry cleaning because he happened to be passing by the place where he knew she took her dresses. He drove her to her parents' to pick up a sofa. He did a lot of picking up and dropping off of things for her, actually. And for a few months, she enjoyed it. He paid for her dinners. He took her to the DMV and then actually waited in line for her while she went to Jamba Juice. Being spoiled rotten by Arman felt pretty good—for a while. But very quickly Marie got bored. Arman always agreed with her, never challenged her, never even pushed to see a different movie now and then. More impor-

The Myth of the "Good Guy"

The Good Guy embarrasses me, and I would like to add as well that he's also beginning to make me mad.... This is not an actual man, it's a counterfeit. You can tell because he walks around all day long with his capital letters showing. "I am the Good Guy," he tells you with every move he makes. "See how I pull out your chair. See me smile appreciatively as you talk, nodding from time to time. See me consider my responses to you, seriously and thoughtfully, turning my head occasionally to let you see the creases forming in my brow.... How I appear is what matters. Roses are red, violets are blue, swallow my story and I love you."

Then there's the good guy—the genuine article who does exist and is the joy of softball teams and bars and dogs and children and, occasionally, you. Because all the things GG puts on, this man just naturally does and is. He pulls out your chair because you personally would like that, probably. He will agree with you because he likes you and thinks you're right, as indeed he will disagree with you because he likes you and thinks you're wrong. If he decides to make a tremendous pass at you, it will be because he'd like to and figures it's up to you, not him, to decide whether it's a good thing to do. Because he is—you should pardon the expression—his own man.

—JAKE, 1967

(including, yes, putting the toilet seat down) and let the dumb stuff slide. And now when I visit home, and my dad gives me his jacket, opens the car door and throws his arm across me if we stop short . . . well, that's just a nice, safe-feeling thing I enjoy with my dad, a man who, by the way, is not my partner in life like Jon is."

Remember that dinner where P met Lily? All Lily saw that night was a dashing P, rising to his feet when she went to the bathroom in a very exhibitionistic show of politesse. But freeze the scene and you'll see, sitting on the other side of the table from Lily, another guy who was invited that night, a brown-haired guy named Lance. Lance is an Invisible Type. You won't see him showing off—he's the kind of man who assumes every woman can see through that crap. You'll see Lance actually *listening* to what other people are saying rather than just waiting for his time to talk.

The truth is there's no shortcut to understanding a man's character. You have to get to know a man to get to know a man.

Lance is handsome, but not the kind of handsome you notice right away. He's the kind of guy who gets better-looking the longer you know him. In fact, Lily didn't notice him at all that night. But she noticed him later—after Lance started dating Lily's friend. That's when Lily got to know him and realized she felt jealous of her friend. "Why can't I meet a good guy like that?" Lily complained to me once. "Why do I have to meet guys like P instead?"

I have to admit it felt pretty good to tell her she *had* met Lance. She just hadn't been looking for him. Lily's jaw dropped. She felt totally embarrassed. It was a flash in which certain parts of her personality were totally illuminated to her for the first time. She was pretending she wanted one type of guy (a good guy, a substantial guy, a guy who's more than just surface), but she actually went for exactly the opposite. These Invisible Types are everywhere, and you hardly ever recognize them until your friend is dating one and then he's not invisible anymore. I'm talking about guys who might be handsome but are a little shy about the fact. Who don't dress to outdo anyone. Who might not insist on getting you a drink when yours is empty (a little too forward, a little too show-offy) but, when he notices you shivering, may ask the bartender if he could turn down the AC. If you're looking for Mr. Invisible, try this next time you're at a party or a club: Freeze the scene, mute the volume and look around. That way you won't be tricked by the guy who's talking the most, or the guy who's ordering the $200 bottle of Champagne to be delivered to his table. See who you're attracted to *then*. See who's actually doing something kind, who's got something deep and interesting in his eyes, although you didn't notice because you were blinded by Mr. Hipster or Mr. Table Service.

The other trick? Try the listening test. Tell a guy a story. Come back to him half an hour later and see if he remembers the main point of it. If you were complaining about someone at work, ask him later what he thinks you should do about it. Or if you'd been talking about your vacation, ask him later if he's ever been somewhere similar. The minute details aren't that important; it doesn't matter if he got your dog's name right or that your vacation was in Cuernavaca. But see if he remembers what you were trying to tell him—that you have serious emotions about your pets, or that you love the beach. If he cares, the important stuff will stick.

Note: The Invisible Type can be hard to approach at a bar, and if you're traveling with a posse of girlfriends, forget about it. Anywhere else, though, all you have to do is ask him a question. And asking a question is really getting to the heart of what this chapter is about. In order to avoid guys like P, or other manipulator types, you have to be able to see through the smokescreens and find out who the guy you're out with really is. Because *that's* the guy you're going to be living with when all the fantasy and gestures start to fade. So make sure you like what's under the shiny armor.

Three Genuinely Chivalrous (and Powerfully Seductive) Things You Can Do for Him

No one's expecting you to take off your coat and throw it across a puddle for him (that would be weird on so many levels), but any of these heartfelt little actions show us you really care.

Tell us you like our shoes.

We know you don't like the way we dress, and that you're always wanting to take us shopping. But if you compliment us when we make a *good* fashion choice, that'll give us more confidence to go out and meet all your well-dressed friends. Bonus: It'll also make us easier to shop with, because we'll think we're doing it together instead of being told what to do.

Give us something just because, with no strings attached.

It could be anything, really: a book you think we'll like (even though you wouldn't be caught dead reading it yourself); more memory for our computer, which is always fritzing out on us (even though you wish we'd spend less time in front of the screen); or, say, a blow job (even though we're about to run out the door, and there's no time for us to return the favor). Here's another great example from 2009 Jake: "My brother had been cooped up in his apartment all weekend, working to meet a deadline, when he received a text from his girlfriend: 'Look outside yr door.' He did, and found a basket of snacks and energy drinks. She was long gone, and when he called to tell her to come back, she refused, saying, 'Finish up so we can play later.' He insists it's the most romantic thing a woman has ever done for him."

Don't watch us try to set up the new flat-screen TV.

We know we're supposed to know how to do that. And yet we don't. We'll figure it out. Just pretend that you have total confidence in our abilities, and leave the room.

Rule #5

Please Don't Pretend to Know What the Infield Fly Rule Is

How to Be Your Most Genuine Self with Him—Because Guys Want You to Be You

f you're like me, Rule #5 will, at times, seem like wishful thinking. A little hokey. Like something Mister Rogers would have said. *All you have to do is be yourself!* (Maybe a more fun way to say it is: No one likes a phony.)

But let me tell you a story that helped me come around to believing it pretty powerfully. About midway through my stint as Jake, I got into a long, drawn-out argument with Genevieve, my long-time editor; like, *really* drawn out—I think it lasted for three months. Writing (and editing) a column like Jake makes you get all existential about sex and love. And I was particularly angsty on the day I e-mailed Genevieve threatening to resign the column. "This is pointless," I wrote. "I hope I'm not being rash, but I feel like I should quit being Jake." Her response: "Why are you being such a drama queen?" I wrote back something about how men weren't worth analyzing—all there was to know was that we could be played like pianos; just press the right keys to get the response you want. "We're either suckers who get manipulated or we're manipulators ourselves," I wrote. "There's no in-between." That's when Genevieve picked up the phone and called me: "Dude," she said, "what *happened*?"

I couldn't take dating anymore, I told Genevieve on the phone. I couldn't stand it. Blossoms and I had been broken up for a month or two, and I'd been seeing a woman I'd met at an Irish pub. She liked to drink whiskey, smoke cigars (holy crapola, am I glad *that* trend is over) and tell stories about her "insane" job on Wall Street. She was just the kind of ballsy, brazen woman I knew I was supposed to find irresistible. And for about five dates, I did. Then one morning, when I woke up and found her making eggs, wearing only my suit jacket (seriously), I just wanted to grab it off her and run out the door. She looked incredibly hot, in a *9½ Weeks* kind of way, but everything about her seemed inauthentic, staged. Suddenly, I couldn't believe I'd been seduced by a girl who smoked cigars. I hate cigars. Later I concluded: There was just no way I could give anyone advice if I was as lost as I felt.

Genevieve tried to reassure me that my callowness in falling for an image that may as well have been invented by the editors of *Maxim* magazine was normal, and that I'd grow out of it: "You fell for an idea, not a person," she said. "Women make the same mistake all the time." I told her that was my point exactly! How was I going to help them when I couldn't even help myself? She told me about a Matthew McConaughey wannabe she'd once been smitten with because he was hot, rich, took her to Atlantic City and called her his Lady Luck.

"His Lady Luck?" I asked. "You heard that and didn't throw up in your mouth a little?"

"I know!" said Genevieve. "I don't even like gambling! And he *so* wasn't my type! But he was very . . ."

"Sexy?" I offered.

"Yeah," said Genevieve. "Sexy but wrong, wrong, wrong, so it wouldn't have lasted, even if he hadn't dumped me. And thank God he did, or I might not have met Ted."

Ted was (and, eight years later, still is, I'm happy to report) Genevieve's husband. At the time, she and I were in totally different places in our lives. I was freshly broken up with Blossoms, a woman it was dawning on me I was in love with. Genevieve was a newlywed. All I really knew about her husband up until that point was that he'd renovated their apartment with his own two hands. (And when I heard that, I felt especially depressed: If finding true love required even knowing how to put an Ikea Hemnes bookshelf together, things did not look good for me!) But on the phone that rainy afternoon, she told me about what had made him fall for her, and her for him.

It was summer. They'd gone on a couple of casual dates, but they'd never even kissed. Then she invited him to spend the weekend at the beach house she shared with a bunch of her friends, Ivy League grads who had oodles of money and owned their own companies and liked to eat lobster and drink prosecco. "A slightly intimidating crowd," Genevieve told me. "But I'd known them forever and loved them." What she hadn't realized until Ted's visit, however, was that she (who was neither rich nor an Ivy girl) acted like a different person around her beach house friends than she did in her normal life. Nervously trying to impress Ted that weekend, she dressed to the nines to go to the beach, dished and name-dropped, and basically came on like a Gossip Girl on steroids. Ted was standoffish the whole time, as if unsure what to make of her and the whole scene. Finally, on his last evening there, Ted pulled her away from the dinner table and took her for a walk on the beach. "If you would just be yourself," he said, "I would be yours." That was all it took, Genevieve told me. From then on, she stopped trying to impress her friends or Ted or anyone else for that matter. She had found her real power in love, and she was exuberantly (if somewhat annoyingly) happy.

I was glad Genevieve hadn't blown it with her rugged-but-sensitive guy—but at that moment in my life, her story seemed a little too good to be true. I couldn't imagine telling a woman, "Just drop the act already, honey," and not getting slapped across the face. In fact, I'm still not really sure how Ted pulled that one off. I agreed with both of them, though, that when you want someone for keeps, you have no choice but to show them your true self, and to insist that they show theirs.

What Genevieve was saying spoke to my situation at the time too, and it might speak to yours. I was being driven crazy by fakeness. Especially a certain kind of fakeness that women try to pull off way too often. You probably know someone who does it. It might even be you! I'm talking about the girl in every crowd who claims to love Ultimate Fighting and beer pong, who makes too big a point of telling you how she eats cold pizza for breakfast and orders her steaks bloody. Or the woman who claims to live for football season (though she doesn't actually know what pass interference looks like) or pornography (though she doesn't actually watch it). A girl who seems to be saying, "I'm one of the guys!"

I don't know how women got the idea that this is what men want in women.

Sure, I love the notion of women letting down their ladylike airs and doing shots of Jack Daniel's sometimes. And it's fun to get carnal on a steak. But acting like a dude is by no means a universal turn-on. We don't want to date one of the guys. If we wanted to date one of the guys, we would be gay, and probably not the most suitable mate for you. Bottom line: Girls who are into sports or cars or booze are cool. Girls who aren't are *also* cool. Girls who aren't but pretend that they are: *not* cool.

It's all about, for lack of a better expression, keeping it real. Back at the time of my conversation with Genevieve, I was despairing that there was such a thing as *real* interaction in the world of dating. But her story about Ted changed my attitude just enough. It also, of course, made me long for Blossoms; we knew each other so well that neither of us would have had much luck being fake with the other.

I was reminded of that lesson not long ago when Blossoms and I went on a kind of double date with my friend Zach. The New York Mets were in the playoffs that year, and we all decided to go watch the game at this little bar/restaurant in the West Village, in Manhattan. Zach and I are die-hard Mets fans—devoted, passionate, eternally pessimistic and beleaguered, as Mets fans should be. Zach's date, Sasha, knew this about him (since it's hard to know

Zach *without* knowing it). We all installed ourselves at the bar, and within about five minutes, I wanted to drive Sasha out to Queens and drop her off at (now the former) Shea Stadium so she could enjoy the Mets up close—and we could watch in peace. She was trying to out-fan us. She called all the players by their first names (and got some of them wrong). Every other sentence, she declared someone the best shortstop in history, or announced that someone else should retire. She would argue with every comment I made about the game, clearly to show off about how well she knew baseball—which she didn't actually know that well.

It was obvious that Sasha was taking a little bit of knowledge, and a normal measure of interest in a hometown baseball team, and trying to make herself into a super-fan. She thought she was going to seduce Zach by being one of the guys. But her technique backfired, because it was so obviously just that: a technique. I saw something change in Zach during that game—an almost physical stiffening—and I knew that he wouldn't go out with Sasha again.

So hear this, women: Be yourself! We *like* that you're different from us. We don't want you to be one of the guys, we just want you to appreciate our guy-ness. And we want you to let us in on what makes you female—whether you're super-girly, a tomboy, or somewhere in between. That worked on 2010 Jake, who wrote after one particularly good date: "She could talk about anything. From whiskey to Lady Gaga. She could dish about the lowbrow (*Jersey Shore*) and the high (the vacation she wanted to take to Tuscany). I was left feeling like she was a woman who is neither stuck-up nor uncivilized. I was crazy about her."

After all, half the fun of being a straight guy is how weird and confounding and totally *other* you women are. Your vernacular and even the way you argue is totally foreign to us. Sure, that some-times leads to frustration. But the gap between us is also a huge part of what makes dating you so great. We love getting to know your smell and your clothes and your grooming habits. We love how opening your medicine cabinet feels like finding a portal to a different world. We love how you wind that stretchy thing into your hair seventeen times in four seconds to make a ponytail. We love everything about you that makes you a little exotic and un-knowable to us.

And that's why there's no need, *ever*, to kiss a guy's blue-jeaned back end. A little enthusiasm for the stuff we love—keg beer, mov-ies with zombies or robots, the Bloomin' Onion, the PlayStation platform, sleeping until noon, and so on—will do just fine.

Here's how Jake described the balancing act in 1976:

Should you be expected to try to like what a man likes? . . . It's a yes and no.

No: You aren't required to admire the line play of the Oakland Raiders . . . or the fact that three of his friends can each balance a pitcher of beer on their chests while singing all 30 verses of "Abdul Abulbul Amir." . . .

But yes: You owe it to yourself to delve into just what it is that makes him like all those strange things, and to be ready, as well, to embrace such of them as you're able to, if you see good reason. . . .

What it comes down to, again, is the difference between tol-erance, a kind appreciation for something whose charms may otherwise be lost on you, and flat-out faking it. Faking it—whether we're talking a knowledge of sports or, slightly unrelated, an orgasm—always comes back to haunt you.

Working It Means Being Yourself

Midway through my Jake tenure, I got the following letter from *Glamour* reader Jacqueline, from California: "Dear Jake, what is the hottest car I can buy that will get guys to notice me?"

My answer to Jacqueline was this: What kind of car do you like? Because that's the only thing that should matter. What kind of car turns *you* on? That's the right car to turn (the right) guys on too.

No matter how much attention you might get (and fun you might have) playing a part—the super-flirt, the guy's gal, the vixen, the hot chick in the Mustang—always remember that the secret to finding *true* power in relationships will never lie in pretending to be someone you're not. Sure, you need to work what you've got (see Jake's Rule #2). But focus on the parts of yourself that make you *you*.

Jake said this in 1956, and it holds true today: "I think it behooves you girls every once in a while to stand off and take a look at yourselves. If it turns out, in all honesty, that you are a real Bohemian type, or a real brain, or a real anything else, then I say great, and Godspeed!" (I don't know that we say "Godspeed" much anymore, but you know what he means.) 1956 Jake continued, "There are plenty of men around who'll find you the perfect companion. But if it turns out that your heart really isn't in the game the way you're playing it, then I say cease and desist. Back up and start over. If there is one characteristic that makes a girl attrac-

tive to men, it's genuineness . . . sincerity. It's the art of being
yourself."

Let me tell you the story of Amanda. In the year 2000, I had a
big New Year's Eve party. It was probably the biggest party I've
ever had. One famous person was there. A short famous person
who is an outspoken vegetarian and isn't even that famous—that's
all I'm telling you. It was the party where someone put my alarm
clock in the microwave, and the floor ended up shellacked in a disgusting mixture of beer and mojito that never really came off. I didn't
know half the people there, and at one point someone actually
asked me to leave because it was getting too crowded.

I do remember wondering, about an hour into the night,
where exactly Amanda was. I'd been dating her for the last month,
and I wasn't really sure where it was going. I liked her—she was a
hyper-smart grad student and had enlightened me, over several
dinners, about a crazy assortment of subjects, from agave farm-
ing to China's propaganda system. But she also intimidated me,
and by the time it occurred to me that she wasn't at the party, I was
already getting some seriously flirtatious vibes from a woman in a
tight blue dress who looked as if she did *a lot* of yoga, and, well, that
could have been that. But then I spotted Amanda. She was sitting
on the sofa, in the middle of the chaos, reading a book. Like, someone was actually shaking his ass in her face—the whole apartment
was a dance floor—while she sat there and read *Drown* by Junot
Díaz, which she'd apparently brought with her. *To a New Year's
party!* (I remember her reading choice clearly, since it was part of
her nerd charm.) From across the room, I studied her long, dark
hair and clear, pale skin. She was totally engrossed in the words
in front of her. She was also wearing a lowish-cut blouse, so there

was a hint of sexuality there (again, Rule #2). I decided at that moment: This could very well be my dream girl.

If Amanda had worked it in some way that contradicted who she really was—if she'd worn a shiny halter top or tried to do the booty-grinding dance—I probably would've cut my losses and turned my attention to Ms. Yoga. But there she was, reading a book in the middle of a New Year's party, seeming more *her* than she'd ever seemed. It was a kind of provocation, and in retrospect, it was unwittingly one of the most brilliant dude-seducing maneuvers I've ever seen, even if she hadn't intended it to be.

When I approached her, I didn't have to think up something artificial to say. That's always seemed impossible to me anyway— sounding natural when striking up a conversation with someone you're attracted to but have no idea where you stand with. All I said was, "Are you really reading *Drown* in the middle of a New Year's party?" As an answer, she reached up, took hold of my collar, pulled me down and kissed me. I basically fell in love with her at that moment. We had two weeks of almost supernaturally good sex and possibly even better conversation, and then she told me that she had gotten back together with her ex-fiancé, which is partly why she didn't end up being my dream girl after all. But she *could* have been, and it all started with her being herself.

Jake gets a lot of letters from readers who want to know how to get a guy friend to see them as something more. This rule is great for that. Take Mazanga, from Maryland, who wrote: "I have a friend and I really like him as more than a friend. He works at the gym I attend, so I see him five days a week, and we enjoy talking to each other. I really want this to lead to a relationship, but he's mysterious, good at hiding his feelings. How do I get him to show me his feelings and be more than friends?" My answer to Mazanga: Show him who *you* are. Broadcast your personality. If you're a nerd, let your nerd flag fly. If you're a Goth girl, raise up that black flag high and proud. If, in your heart of hearts, you are happiest shaking your ass on the dance floor like a Michigan State freshman on spring break—by all means, do that. Sometimes you have to *show off* who you are for the right guy to pick up on it. Had Amanda merely been making polite conversation with someone at the edges of that party, things probably wouldn't have heated up with us the way they did that night. Bottom line: Even if you're being yourself, you sometimes need to do it in a slightly louder way to get dumbasses like me to stop staring at famous vegetarians.

You might be wondering, *What's the difference between Amanda and Mets Girl, Jake's friend's date from earlier in this chapter?* My answer: Amanda was just amplifying who she really was, while Mets Girl was pretending to like the Mets because that's what she thought guys liked. Can you see how one of those women was finding her secret power and the other one is . . . Mets Girl?

In the end, it all boils down to those two very powerful words: Be yourself.

The Dos and Don'ts of Living in Guy World

Here are six things you absolutely shouldn't bother doing to impress, or fit in with, the man you're seeing:

- **Don't** fearlessly follow your boyfriend on a double-black-diamond ski run if you're actually crapping your ski pants. **Do** admit that you're terrified of black diamonds—and promise to crush him later at Ping-Pong.

- **Don't** act like you drink straight tequila if smelling straight tequila brings you back to that time you barfed through your nose at that frat party in college. **Do** realize you can just say, "I'm not drinking tonight." (It's a good phrase to know.)

- **Don't** act like it's no big deal to go skinny-dipping if it actually makes you embarrassed and uncomfortable. **Do** take as much off as you're comfortable with, and have some good, clean, wet fun.

- **Don't** fake a deep love for KFC if you're a member of PETA. **Do** fake a deep love for his mom's cooking, or at least refrain from making gagging motions the first time you eat dinner at her house.

- **Don't** act enthusiastic about doing sexual things you've never done, never wanted to do, and would prefer to do later, much later, or possibly never. **Do** let him know when he can help fulfill something you *have* always wanted to try.

- **Don't** pretend you're one of those girls who doesn't care about clothes if you really have a closet the size of his living room. **Do** let it roll off your back when he teases you about having a closet the size of his living room.

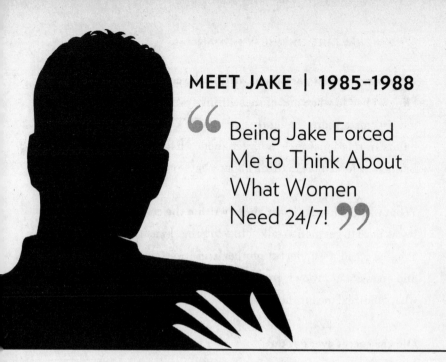

MEET JAKE | 1985–1988

" Being Jake Forced
Me to Think About
What Women
Need 24/7! "

*In this Jake's day, Madonna ruled the airwaves and big hair was the
bomb. Having previously written about ethics for a major men's magazine, Reagan-era Jake often tackled moral issues in Glamour—but
never in a finger-wagging way. In columns like "Is There a Nice Way to
Say No?" he made his case that strong women finish first in love.*

How did being Jake change you?

I was Jake twenty-five years ago, and at that time it helped me realize how much of a hunger there was for young women to have
men talk to them seriously about relationships, about sex, about
what the world looks like from a male perspective.

What was the best part about writing the column?

I knew I had to write one of these things every month, so it made me become a more thoughtful person. It's easy to fall into lazy habits in relationships—to forget about what other people need. Being Jake forced me to think about what women need 24/7!

What was the hardest part about writing the column?

It was hard to get men to talk! I like to think I wasn't like this personally; I had a wonderful mother and I was always very chatty and open about my own emotions. I like to think that was part of what qualified me for the job of Jake.

Did the secret ever get out?

Not in any public way. The Internet didn't exist then, otherwise I'm sure it would have.

What was the most profound thing you learned about men?

Men, I learned, didn't tend to talk about their feelings very much. And that caused a lot of frustration in the women they knew. But men themselves could *also* be frustrated at their inability to talk about these things. I tried to explain that to women—they *want* to be communicative, they just don't know how.

And about women?

I learned nothing about women! I still know nothing! But I will say this, and I don't know how to say this in a politically correct way, but I came to feel that a great many women are terribly insecure—about relationships, about their own desirability.

Did you ever find true love?

Yes, I did. I met my wife two or three years after I gave up the Jake column and married her three years after that. I'm very happily married. It came out at some point that I had been Jake, and my wife thought it was amusing. But she never felt she had to go back and read the old columns to figure me out.

Do you think the dating landscape has changed since you were Jake?

I'd like to think that men and women talk more openly now. That they're more honest with each other. And more honest about the premises of what they're after—that there's less of an emphasis on coolness and more of an emphasis on finding someone with some substance.

Don't Sleep with Him Too Soon!

How to Make a Real Sexual Connection, but Not Before You're Ready

Okay, women: We've arrived at the sex chapter. But don't worry: Contrary to the title of this one, I'm not going to give you some morally righteous lecture about what you should and shouldn't do with your bodies. I know better than that! I'm well aware that I'm talking to the most sexually empowered generation of women in history, and for the most part, you're having sex because you love your bodies and love men's bodies. Because it just plain feels good. Because you *own* your desires! And hey, that's fantastic for everyone involved. But it's not enough if you want to be truly empowered in love. If you want to take *real* control of your romantic future, you need to know this: *It's okay to admit that you want more than a sexual connection from the guys you date.*

And how do you get more? Don't sleep with him too soon. Yes, it's a generalization. A generalization that *works*.

Here's a little story from back when I was single. One night I was sitting at home in my apartment, watching *Reservoir Dogs* for the thirty-seventh time. Just as I was starting to realize that thirty-seven is too many times to watch *Reservoir Dogs* if you want to find it entertaining, I got a text from Nell, a girl who lived almost exactly across the street from my building. It said, "I'm horny and bored." Nell was a friend of a friend, and we'd run into each other a few times in the neighborhood. She was slight, with a pixie haircut and a punk-rock sense of style. We had an openly flirty rapport, but she'd always had a boyfriend, so nothing had ever come of it.

This time it was about to. I texted back that her condition sounded dire, and I'd do whatever I could to help her out. Within twenty minutes, Nell was in my apartment. Which, I have to say, was totally weird. I realized, as she leaned back suggestively on my bed, that (1) she'd never been in my apartment before, nor I in hers; (2) there was no question what was going to transpire—no more question than if I were a gigolo—which kind of took the suspense and energy out of the whole thing; and (3) I had no real idea why she wanted to have sex with me.

We tried to get a little drunk first—we were both obviously feeling awkward—but I didn't feel like chugging four beers and then hopping in the sack and trying not to barf. So we just did it. It wasn't the worst sex I'd ever had in my life. But let's just say it wasn't the most awesome, either. And about an hour from the time she'd sent that original text, she was gone. A few months later, we ran into each other buying iced coffee at our local café, and I walked her home.

"You're the most modern woman I know," I told her. "At least sexually speaking."

"Yeah, well," said Nell, "I was with my ex for, like, ten years. So I guess I'm trying to make up for lost time. Since I broke up with him, I've been a totally different person. I want to be able to have insane, intense, random sex and not feel bad about it."

Then she told me that her plan wasn't going that well. Having sex with people she barely knew hardly packed any emotional punch at all. And she'd always been a sucker for emotional punch, or at least a little of the drawn-out sexual tension that comes from waiting to have sex with someone you're attracted to. As we sat on her front steps, she told me that I seemed like the kind of guy she'd like to date, but that the spell had been broken by our mediocre sex, and she was now sleeping with a different possibly-right-for-her guy whom she'd met at a dance party. I remember thinking, *Whoa, this girl is way more confident and attractive just sitting here talking to me than she was in my bedroom, trying to imitate Sharon Stone in* Basic Instinct.

And then, *Whoa, it's kind of sad that she doesn't realize that.*

Of course, that realization shouldn't have surprised me. At that moment in my life as Jake, I was deluged with letters from women who were trying to be casual about sex when they didn't actually *feel* that casual. For months I'd been a little heartbroken over those letters. I'd heard from women who thought that by asking for more than sex from a guy, they were being high maintenance; women who believed that if they didn't give the men they were dating what they wanted sexually, they'd lose them; women who'd tried to sleep their way to intimacy with men and failed; women who, like Nell, thought that having quick, meaningless sex would make them feel powerful, but then found out it made them feel the opposite.

There was Katie, from Nebraska, who'd written: "I've been spending a lot of time with this guy who just moved to town. The sex is amazing! But I'm really confused. It's like he's undecided about me or something. He'll ask me to come over and spend the night almost every night, but other times he asks me to go home. Is he just unsure of how he feels or is he using me?"

And then there was Alex, from Ohio, who e-mailed: "I've always been the 'friend with benefits' and never the actual girlfriend, so I never know if a guy really, truly likes me when we hook up. How can I tell?"

And I'd gotten *lots* of mail like this, from Chasity, in Missouri: "I've been having a sexual relationship for three years with a guy who won't commit. I try not to expect too much of him, but I want more. What should I do?"

What *should* Chasity do? And Katie? And Alex? I told them what I would've told Nell if she'd asked me: *Not only is it okay to tell a guy you want more than a sexual connection, it's completely necessary!* And while you're at it, ladies, go ahead and free yourself from the "If I really want this guy, I'd better be 100 percent sexually available to him right away" mind-set. We're not in high school anymore, and you shouldn't be ruled by the fear of losing a guy because you don't put out. Again, I fully realize that lots of you— probably most of you—*aren't* just "putting out." You're having sex for the very same reasons men do: because it's fun; because it's a great stress reliever; because it's a way of connecting with the mysterious opposite sex; and because, whether we like to admit this or not, *damn*, it's a rush to turn another human being into a hungry, quivering, irrational (yet exceedingly complimentary) animal.

But that said, all of the above is, remarkably, not all that empowering, no matter what sex you are. One day you realize emotionless sex makes you feel more lonely instead of less. You figure out that calling the shots in the bedroom isn't all that independent if the person you're with calls them *outside* of it; that commanding a booty call with a tap of your iPhone is not the same as commanding someone's respect. Furthermore, being a friend with benefits isn't actually all that modern after all (Henry VIII and Cleopatra had lots of casual lovers, did they not?). And, face it, you don't *want* to be a friend with benefits. If all you wanted to be was a friend with benefits, you wouldn't need this book. You want more. You deserve more. So here are four steps to help you claim your sexual power (perhaps the most beguiling of all your powers, by the way).

1) Like I said, don't have sex too soon. At the risk of sounding like a fuddy-duddy, the secret is in these three words: *What's the rush?* This isn't a moralistic question. I'm not saying you have to abide by some arbitrary rule: I don't believe that waiting for the fourth date, or the fifth date, or the one-month mark makes a person any more admirable, impressive or worthy. What I do think is that sex with someone you have something invested in actually *feels* better. There are so many steps to savor: the moment when you know you want him; the moment when you *almost* succumb to the desire but decide to hold out just a little longer; the many moments of pent-up desire in the meantime; and then the good three months of doing nothing but indulging in that desire. Wouldn't it suck to skip those? You don't eat your Halloween candy all at once, do you? Or, rather, when you ate your Halloween candy all at once that time when you were eleven years old, weren't you disappointed and depressed that you had nothing to look forward to? Not to mention, kind of nauseous and acne-ed? But I digress. The point is, don't rush through that insane early period of getting to know someone you're into. If a guy's worth your while, he'll wait for you. And waiting will only *enhance* his interest.

Just ask Blossoms. She made us wait many, many dates into our relationship (well, actually, she said she wanted to wait and then changed her mind, by which time I'd decided *I* wanted to wait to prove I was a gentleman). The point being: By the time we finally did it, I was so head-over-heels for her I couldn't even see straight. And yes, that made it better. So much better than it would've been if we'd ripped each other's clothes off after our first great date and second bottle of wine. I'm so glad we got to savor all those moments of pure, unconsummated attraction—not only are they rare and powerful and a huge turn-on, but they're also the moments when you figure out who this person is that you're attracted to. And by the time Blossoms and I spent the night together, I was hooked—completely hooked—on that person.

What we got, ultimately, by waiting was a richer, rawer, sexier sex life. (And a period of insanely nutty, great sex.) But many women don't wait. That's understandable (it's sex, after all!), but that's also sometimes a shame—because it can keep you from looking at the big picture with a man.

The big picture is something my friend Nicky, from college, was never much good at paying attention to. By the time we were in our late twenties, I'd watched her botch the sex part of her relationships for a decade. She's the kind of woman who was always having casual sex with some guy who never seemed to be around, and about whom she didn't feel that *casual*. Until something snapped. Nicky had been dating a man who kept things "light" with her for three months—and, then, out of the blue, she found out that he'd gotten engaged to another woman. To her own surprise, she was devastated; that night, she cried herself to sleep. In the morning, Nicky woke up and wrote some new rules of her own. She decided that the next time she was feeling insecure with a guy, she would not throw her body at him; she would sleep on that feeling—to make sure she still felt something significant the next time she saw him, and the next, and the next. Only when she felt strongly that her attraction to him went deeper than the physical (and vice versa), would she act on it. A year later Nicky found herself in a committed relationship with a really good guy. And the sex is apparently more intense and kinky than the kind she'd had on any of her supposedly exciting one-night stands. As Nicky put it the other day, "You have to ask yourself: 'Who is this person I'm having sex with?' If you don't really know, he's probably feeling the same way. And how can the two of you really respect each other if you don't know each other? Believe me, when a guy really gets you, judgment goes out the window. You can be 100 percent yourself sexually, and he'll only think more of you for it."

Yep, the first step to having a rocking sex life is waiting to have sex until you're with a guy who truly deserves to put his hands on your body. How will you know when you've found him? I wish I could say there was a golden rule to go by, but all I can say is that it's about knowing yourself. Oh, all right, I do have a little test that worked for me back when I was single and trying to learn how to think with my heart instead of my . . . yes, that. Want to try it? Close your eyes and imagine yourself going home and having (safe!) sex with this bewitching person tonight. Okay, now imagine the "after" part—not how you fantasize it will be, but how you can really picture it going: Are you comfortable walking around naked in front of your new lover? Which do you feel more: relaxed and confident—or anxious and insecure? I think you know what the correct answers are. If you trust yourself, and this dude, enough to have answered them with extreme confidence . . . well, some guy's about to get lucky tonight.

Oh, and a P.S.: Don't hit on new guys through e-mail or text. Those shortcuts allow you to say, and propose, all kinds of things way too soon. Believe me, I've sent e-mail come-ons to women I never would have come on to in person, and the results weren't good.

2) Now that you're a couple, keep flipping the script. From Jake's experience, nothing keeps a relationship going stronger than a sex life that grows—and changes—as the two people in charge of it do.

Another way of saying that? Stagnation equals death. No one wants to have the same sex with the same person over and over and over again for the rest of his or her life. Especially not men, who can suffer from a bit of the old penis wanderlust even in the best of circumstances. Change is the friend of a healthy, fun, satisfying sex life. Not change you're truly uncomfortable with, though. You don't have to feel pressured to mix things up by bringing home your party-girl work colleague who's been hinting about how cute your boyfriend is and how much she loves threesomes (though, if you've always wanted to try one, okay!). I think of sex the way I think of working out. I'm one of those people who has to switch up what I do for exercise once in a while or I'll go nuts. When I get sick of running, I'll try yoga. When that starts to feel like a chore, I'll start getting into weight training. That way I'm always excited about it. Sex should be like that too. It should be experimental, exploratory. What if I put my mouth here? What if I flirted with someone else in a bar beforehand, just to set the mood? What if she wore a wig?

Men love a woman who's a little unpredictable in bed. And once we're on solid footing with her *outside* the bedroom, we even like it when she's a *lot* unpredictable. If one night she uses us like a personal sex treadmill and the next she plays the part of the pure maiden, we're down with that. So indulge the opposites within yourself—your take-me-in-the-elevator side *and* your treat-me-like-a-lady side. Hey, if you feel like it, you can even be both kinds of lover on the same night.

This advice can be passed along to your guy, too: Aren't you tired of the way he always asks for a blow job by lying back on the pillows and giving you that look? Or the fact that he uses his hand exactly the same way whenever he performs certain anatomical tasks? Don't you want him to talk dirty now and then? Or treat you with a hint of playful roughness? Or insist that tonight only *you* will be pleased? The problem with men is that they can be very demanding when it comes to sex, but not very imaginative. Most of the time, it's a question of simply letting him know you want something different. When men get into a rut, they sometimes forget that there are options. It's a failure of the imagination. So tell us what you want! Just know we're a little sensitive, so instead of saying, "I'm sick of X," try, "I've been dreaming of you doing Y to me all day, and now I want it."

And what if you're lucky enough to be with a guy who *is* imaginative? Go along with it. Maybe you'll learn you actually like something that you hated with your last guy. Maybe you'll discover you're less shy than you thought. Maybe you'll acquire a taste for something you never even dreamed of doing—'til you tried it. As a wise friend of mine once said, "I hate olives, but I try them once every three years to see if I'm still right that I hate them."

Now, if you know that you (metaphorically speaking) despise olives and always will, you don't have to follow my friend's example. But if a man proposes you eat some olives (metaphorically speaking, people) with him in bed, don't make him feel like a deviant, and don't just shut him down without at least talking about it. I remember telling a woman I dated that I wanted to get naked and give her a foot massage, and she told me that feet are disgusting and repulsive in general. It definitely killed the mood, and it also made me reluctant to order anything else that was not on the regular menu with her. I'm not saying I needed her to be into feet. I just wanted her to remember that there were two of us having sex, and we both have desires, so we'd better find a happy medium. No one wants to be in a romantic dictatorship. In fact, I think, as long as he's not asking something of you that feels degrading (in which case, by all means, refuse, and reconsider whether he's the right guy for you), try to be a little flexible. If he gets super turned on by pouring a bottle of baby oil on you, but you don't like how the stuff smells, surprise him with some massage oil that *you* like. Conversely, of course, feel free to gently modify his technique if he's not giving you the right touch. He should be getting off on your pleasure, after all, and you should be getting off on his.

Speaking of getting off, I have something important to say about porn. It seems like it's become a popular way people try to sexually recharge their relationships. And Jake has noticed that more and more women are at least claiming they watch it these days. I think some women think of it as a hip signifier of how modern and empowered they are—kind of like texting a booty call. Well, if you genuinely enjoy looking at it, more power to you. But if you're like some of Jake's female friends, it might not be your cup of tea, and that's okay too! You won't lose any points with a nice dude for saying you'll take a pass. You'll never do yourself any favors by pretending to be someone you're not— you'll just end up watching porn that makes you uncomfortable and pretending you like it. And if you still don't believe that, reread Rule #5: "Please Don't Pretend to Know What the Infield Fly Rule Is."

3) No matter *how* long you've been together, don't spill all your sexual tricks at once. Here's Jake's next golden secret to a long and happy sex life: When it comes to your bag of sexual tricks, you can and should save some for later—like when you've been with a guy for at least a year. Sure, this might be a little manipulative; the promise of something exotic, something kinky, something totally unexpected, will make just about any guy crazy with desire. But the fact that you'll keep him seduced by doing this is just icing on the cake—what Jake is really talking about is respecting yourself and your relationship. Plus, it's much more fun to push boundaries when you actually *have* boundaries.

If you're having a hard time coming up with something to hold out for, use your imagination! You can save having sex in a public space; you can save the experience of putting on a strip-tease for him; you can save going on the Pill instead of using condoms if he proves worthy. As long as you're not faking enthusiasm, setting future dates for new sexual milestones is a great way to keep tension and excitement in the mix.

One caveat: There's a thin line between saving something good for later and withholding. I used to go out with a girl named Angie. She had straight black hair that she cut into a cute bob, deep, dark eyes and perfectly shaped lips. I wanted her terribly all the time. She, however, seemed to enjoy provoking my lust for her more than actually satisfying it. She'd dress super-sexy on dates and make playful suggestions about what she'd like to do to me when we were alone—but once we *were* alone, she'd become aloof, always letting me make the first move. She was joyless and a little calculating about sex. And you know what? That made me want her obsessively. But it also drove me to end the relationship on our six-month anniversary. I told Angie that my longing for her felt like an unpleasant addiction, not love. Probably not the nicest way I've ever broken up with someone, but the truth.

4) Know this: Men aren't going to stop wanting to have sex with other people. Ever. But that doesn't lessen your power. For a long time I lied to Blossoms. Not about anything in particular, but about a thousand things. They were all small, insignificant, and I saw all of them as white lies. (I don't think white lies are always bad, though as I get older, I think they're less and less necessary. They only make the truth that much harder to say later on, when you need to.)

Anyway, one of the things I'd always lied to Blossoms about is having moments when I want to sleep with other women. She knows that all guys check out most women they see (that's Jake 101!). But whenever she asked me if I was attracted to someone we just met at a party, or a woman who was walking down the street, I'd say some form of, *Oh, she's objectively attractive, but she doesn't really do it for me.* Even if she very much did it for me. Blossoms left it well enough alone until one night when we'd been out at a dinner party, and I was especially flirty with a redhead who was the date of a friend. When I denied that I was actually *attracted* to her, Blossoms let me have it. She said it was annoying—I always said the same thing, and it couldn't always be true. Not to mention that she'd been *at the table* and was smart enough to know flirting when she saw it.

Then I got honest as well. I told her she wasn't the easiest person to be straight with when it came to other women. She had a track record of jealousy. And she also had a track record of being a tireless romantic—thinking relationships should hew to Jane Austen plots, and we should feel out-of-control passion for each other at all times and never feel tempted by the charms of others. She admitted it. This is one of my favorite things about Blossoms: not that she is always the perfect wife (how boring would that be?), but that she's honest about herself. Pretty much anything is forgivable if you are able to own your flaws. Then she admitted something else to me: There was a part of her, shut in a dark, locked room she didn't like to open, that was afraid I was going to leave her. And all her jealousy, all the insistence on storybook romance around the clock, was covering up that fear.

"I get scared of you having sex with someone else," she said. "Because every woman is told, from the time she's old enough to understand, that men aren't faithful, that men don't want to have sex with only one woman for the rest of their lives, that every man is terrified on the day of his wedding about all that."

Then, upping the ante still more, I said she was right—at least partially. Men do want to sleep with other women. Just about every man I know feels that way to some extent. (And it's funny, just saying that made me want to do it much less.) It's one of the reasons marriage is such a treacherous endeavor. And it's why you need all the tools possible to make it fun. All that stuff I wrote about before—especially the trying-new-things part, the part where I suggest hitting the sexual reset button every once in a while—is about keeping a relationship sexually exciting. Which is the simplest way to ward off infidelity. But to get back to the point of this book, your power comes from knowing and accepting this. From realizing that honesty helps. From knowing that a relationship needs to continually feel alive, which is another important weapon in the battle for happy, long-term love (which, by the way, is why Rule #1: "Always Hit on the Wingman," isn't just for singles).

Blossoms's secret to tapping into *her* power about all this, which she told me only recently, is deciding that some jealousy—so long as it's not a reaction to any real line-crossing by either of us—is healthy and natural in our relationship. It means we're married to hungry, attractive people. It reminds us that we don't take each other for granted. Now, when Blossoms feels jealous, she knows the most empowering thing she can possibly do is to tell me—in a sharing and nonaccusatory way—exactly how she's feeling. We both know I'd never risk losing her by doing something stupid, and that I'd be too bowled over with guilt to actually enjoy it—but all the same, it can't hurt for me to say that out loud once in a while. In fact, I *like* Blossoms's requests for affirmation. Yes, she needs, occasionally, to hear that I want her and only her. But because she's so calm and straightforward about it, there's nothing needy, anymore, about her.

In the end, the best sexual relationships are the ones in which both partners let themselves be, by turns, powerful *and* vulnerable. That's what makes you hot, and that's what makes us hot. And if you're still not convinced, I leave you with this little tale from 2007 Jake:

One night my date—a pretty real estate agent—bit me. We'd come back to my apartment after seeing a movie and were no sooner in the door than she started kissing my neck and moaning in my ear. It sounded kind of hot but not really genuine, so I pulled away a little. That's when she kissed her way down to my chest and bit my nipple. Hard. "Ow!" I yelped. "You bit me!" I crossed my arms, closing my body off to any further advances. But even though I was the one with a bruised nipple, I started to feel a little guilty: I realized she was only doing what she thought men wanted. . . . [Later], trying to restart our sexual momentum while protecting my flesh, I pulled her onto me. I was amazed at what happened next. "Don't judge," she said. "I've never been on top before." She was a master of pornstar tricks, yet she'd never been in the position even *I* had read was supposed to be the best for women? Once she was there, she was unsure and incredibly attractive—even though the sex was a little awkward. Afterward, she got up and threw on one of my T-shirts. As I watched her, the tee skimming the tops of her naked thighs, I thought, That's *all a man needs.* Sometimes the most effective sex trick is no trick at all.

Jake's Guide to Talking Dirty

There once was a girl named Polly. She was funny and sweet smelling and nice, the kind of girl you make out with for what feels like ten minutes, only to find out it's been two hours. One night, after we'd been dating (and having nice conventional sex) for a while, she came to meet me at a party. It was a work function, filled with people I was uncomfortable around and whom she didn't know at all. I leaned over and kissed her, and she whispered something in my ear that is not printable. And she went on from there. She described scenarios, physical positions, textures, tastes and temperatures in incredible detail. It was possibly the most sexually excited I've ever been with my pants on.

Talking dirty is an essential weapon in anyone's sexual arsenal, one that women are too often scared to use. But it's incredibly easy. And while there's no one way to do it, there are some things that drive most men crazy with desire, and others that drive us just plain crazy. Here are the basics.

Be specific

"I want you" is fine. But "I want you to *bleep* my *blank*," for example, is finer. The idea is to paint a detailed picture for us of how much you like sex. We're very visual creatures, after all.

Use the right words for his private parts

The least risky option is to call it "you." Like "I want you in my ____." A girl isn't going to ruin the moment with that. The most common word for it, which rhymes with *rock*, is what they use in porno movies, so most men have been brainwashed into thinking it's sexy. That works too. But personally, I'd avoid the word that's short for Richard. It's too sixth grade.

Know that timing is everything

It's pretty safe to say outrageously naughty things in the following two situations: if the man is a one-night stand, or if your partner is the kind of guy who'll be able to laugh about it with you later. If he is the latter, then it's a question of finding a time when he both least expects it and also wants it. Picture Polly at my work party. I would have felt differently if we had been sitting at brunch with my parents.

Please don't call it "making love"

Women always say they want to make love when they start talking dirty. What the hell does that mean? Are you inviting us to manufacture love? Is your apartment zoned for that? Do I need to be in some kind of labor union? Remember, part of the exhilaration of dirty talk is to celebrate sex for sex's sake (it just happens to be more fun if you're with someone you love).

Take the ten-minutes-later test

Go ahead, get caught up in the moment. But also remember that orgasm changes everything: If what you're saying will mortify you ten minutes after sex, when you're watching TV in your underwear, don't say it.

Rule #7

Keep Dating Other People Longer Than You Think You Should

Trust Me. It Works. Always.

Yes, I mean what I said in that chapter title up there on the top of the page. You've found a great guy by being yourself, you've resisted the impulse to sleep with him immediately and you've discovered the power that comes with *that*. Now the temptation is to relax—ah! you've got him!—and start couch shopping. Don't. Not yet. Here's why. . . .

My editor Genevieve and I used to meet for monthly lunches at a diner around the corner from the *Glamour* offices. During one meal that I remember vividly, she pointed a Caesar salad–loaded fork at me and said, somewhat angrily, "You know what the problem with women is? We need to be more selfish." I got a little scared. Was she going to stab me with her fork on behalf of womankind?

"What do you mean?" I asked.

"A whole lot of our dating problems could be solved with a little old-fashioned self-interest," Genevieve declared.

"You know," I said, no longer fearing I'd leave lunch with fork marks on my face, "I agree. Men will push the limits. We'll see what we can get away with." It's true. We're like kids—we do better with boundaries. "Give men even the smallest window and we'll be totally self-centered," I said. "That's a huge part of the problem."

"Yep," Genevieve said. "Not one of a man's best qualities. But it's weird how fast a man can shape up if you stand up to him even a little."

She was right. If a man sees that he's with a woman who's clearly looking out for *her* interests? We suddenly become more likely to think about what she needs too.

And I really believe that: Sometimes being powerful means being a little selfish, especially early in a relationship, before you're sure where things are going. I don't mean you should hurt a new boyfriend on purpose or make him watch Jennifer Aniston movies over and over again. I mean you should think about whether a guy is giving you what you need, emotionally and physically, before you close yourself off to the world of *other* guys out there who are probably dying to be with you—especially now that you've tapped into your total amazingness through Jake's rules.

If you've found a guy who is dying to be with you as much as you're dying to be with him—if there's a ring on your finger and a date on the calendar—by all means, skip this chapter. But should there be any doubt that your guy is full-on committed to his relationship with you, then you should really, seriously, follow Rule #7 and *keep your options open*. That means dating other guys, or at least thinking about it—or at least going out once in a while, by yourself or with your single friends, to a place where someone might meet a man—until both you and your main guy feel certain that *this* is the relationship you want above all others, at least for the foreseeable future.

"Why?" some of you may be asking. "Why should I keep dating instead of focusing my energy on getting the guy I really like to commit/get a job/dress better/treat me better?" Or "Why should I keep dating when I *hate* dating and love being in a relationship?" You should keep dating because being scared of dating, if that's your reason, isn't the best reason to stop. You should keep dating because it'll keep you from being a wishful monogamist like my friend Stephanie (more about her in a minute), who's in love with the idea of having a boyfriend rather than in love *with* her boyfriend. And if none of that matters to you, keep doing it because it'll make you more attractive to the guy you like, or at least convince him that he needs to keep his eye on you. Ridiculous but true.

But mostly, keep dating because it's a way of telling yourself, and him, *I deserve to be happy, and I will make sure that I get what I deserve*. And that's power.

Of course, there's a limit to how long a person can keep their options wide open without seriously pissing off some of those options. But there's no hard-and-fast rule about how long that is. Like I said, Rule #7 applies until you're both equally committed to each other. And sorry, but chances are you're going to get there before your guy does (read chapter 9 before you yell at me!), so stick with it until then.

I came to this theory by observation. I watched my friend Amy keep her options open the first month after she met the man she ended up marrying—she said it made her feel less desperate. Melinda, a work colleague, made herself say yes to several dates after she started sleeping with a guy she'd had a massive crush on for years, in order to try to keep perspective; lucky for her, too, because by dating other guys she could see that, by comparison, he wasn't treating her very well. I've even seen it firsthand. I remember dating a woman when I was just out of college, and after our second date she told me that she had a rule: She was still young (twenty-two, I believe), and while she ultimately wanted monogamy, for now she would probably say yes if another guy asked her out. That worked on me because it cast me, easily, as the pursuer rather than the pursued. (Until she moved to San Francisco.)

Is dating around fair? As long as you're being honest, absolutely. But the whole idea is ruined if you're playing cloak-and-dagger with the guys you're dating. The message you want to send him here isn't "I'm not trustworthy"; the message is "I respect myself, I'm an attractive woman, and I have enough self-esteem to believe I deserve to do what I want." So the one thing you shouldn't do is run around behind someone's back. Not that you have to give an exhaustive review of every date you've gone on (that seems kind of sadistic). But under no circumstances should you pretend you're being monogamous if you're not.

The problem you're going to run into, if you're a nice person, is the problem of guilt. Here's what Jake has to say about that: If you're lying, you *should* feel guilty. So don't lie. But never feel guilty for honestly, openly doing what's right for you. Feel *compassionate* if what you're doing is causing your new man friend a little anxiety, but don't feel guilty. In my experience, incidentally, women are far more prone to this kind of guilt than men are, even when the men they're dating haven't shown themselves to be completely committed.

That's like people who feel awful taking new jobs when their old boss won't promote them, because they're worried about hurting their old boss's feelings. My friend Simone is the assistant to an executive, a job she's outgrown, and now she's been recruited to work as a junior executive herself. And she's actually thinking about *not* taking the job because she feels guilty about leaving her boss. That's crazy! And so is not pursuing what's right for you in love just because you don't want to hurt someone's feelings. This, of course, goes way beyond dating. It has to do with how you interact with the world. It's about being good to yourself and honest about what you want. And finally, it's about paying attention to what every grandma since the beginning of time has said: Don't put all your eggs in one basket.

Of all the chapters in this book, this is the one I most want my friend Stephanie to read. I've been friends with Steph for about twenty years. We made out once in college at a Dave Matthews concert (hey, it was the nineties). But other than that, we've been perfectly platonic. During our single years, we turned to each other for straight-up dating advice, and when I was Jake, she became a kind of secret resource. Because I took my anonymity seriously, I didn't tell her about my life as a dating columnist, but listening to her talk about her relationships really helped me understand the way women see the world. In particular, Steph illuminated the fact that women are usually *way* too optimistic about the men they date. You gals can take a few decent gestures from a prospective boyfriend and construct a whole decent person out of them; and, boy, do you have a knack for turning a blind eye to all the red flags that scream "commitment-phobe."

Steph is what I call a "wishful monogamist." The woman is built for monogamy. She loves the trappings of boyfriendhood— the movie nights, the hanging out all Sunday morning in sweat-pants, the researching of bed-and-breakfast getaways. So as soon as she goes on a single date with a guy she likes (in fact, she'll sometimes do this before she's even physically *met* a guy she's been flirting with online), she'll cut off all ties to other single men and start being a girlfriend. Sometimes it scares off possibly good guys. To quote *Wedding Crashers*: "I got a stage-five clinger!" And sometimes guys end up taking long-term advantage of her. Like the guy I nicknamed Teenager Man. The first thing Stephanie said to me when I went to visit her and Teenager Man in Colorado, where they were living together, was "He's not as bad as he seems." Talk about a ringing endorsement. When we walked into the house they shared, Teenager Man just kind of rolled his eyeballs toward me, then rolled them back toward the *World Series of Poker* rerun on ESPN2. When Stephanie brought him a tuna sandwich, he said, "I'm sick of tuna!" and then ate it. Angrily.

But even worse than Teenager Man have been the guys who didn't have the heart to tell Stephanie that they were seeing other people. And still worse yet, she's dated some scumbags who knew that if they acted like a boyfriend once a week or so, she'd be a re-liable and eager booty call.

Stephanie's problem is that she sees the best in people. She's always been like that, about everyone; she believes and is moved by the story of every panhandler she meets on the street, and I

think that's kind of beautiful. But it can be a problematic attri-
bute when it comes to dating. And I don't want to take that away
from her—if I somehow transformed Steph into a cynical person,
I would be extremely depressed. I just want her to take a deep
breath, step away from the dude and, to mix my metaphors, stroll
around and look at some of the other models, even if she thinks
she's found the car she wants. "Easy enough for you to say," Steph
said. "How the hell am I supposed to do that?"

Well, Steph, I'm glad you asked.

Think of It This Way: You're Not Looking for Love, Necessarily— You're Just Getting Out of the House

How the hell do you date other people without pissing off the guy
you're into? A good rule regarding timing: Do it right up until the
point that it even vaguely starts to feel like lying. Then stop. Generally, I think it's fine to date other people for the first two months
in most cases, unless things get really intense, really fast, *for both
of you*. One other important self-check: When you're really honest
with yourself, does your relationship totally qualify as a *relationship*? You know what I mean. Are you both present in each other's
lives, physically and emotionally? If your answer is anything other
than yes, keep dating other people.

The second rule is to be aboveboard about it. You don't have to
rub his face in it; you can be honest and respectful without being
a tease. When my friend Tara needed to tell her almost-boyfriend
that she'd been out with someone else, she said, "I'm really doing

this more for myself, because I tend to overcrowd people, get too intense too fast and make life difficult for myself and the guy I'm dating." He was patient and waited around, so it worked.

And one last—and actually super-important—distinction: I'm not necessarily saying that you *have* to actively date more than one guy. I'm saying don't close yourself off too soon. Go out with your single friends to a bar, without acting like the married lady who's along as the chaperone. Leave your Match.com profile up and active if you've got one. Meet a guy friend for a drink, even if you're not into him. Just don't rule out your options. Give yourself some space to be able to see your love life for what it is, good or bad.

Then, Keep Dating Until You Know If You're with a Type One or a Type Two

There are two kinds of guys who "aren't ready" to commit in my opinion. One will, eventually; the other is a lost cause. They're both perfect candidates for the "keep on dating other people" strategy, because it's going to help you separate one type from the other. And knowing which camp the man you're dating falls into is crucial.

Let's start with the guy I'll call a Type One. The Type One is a guy who is scared to commit. He might be nice and funny and good with your nieces and nephews, he might even be *the one* in some theoretical way. It's just that for him, the idea of being the caretaker of someone's *entire basket of eggs* is terrifying. It makes him sweaty; it makes him want to run away. How do you know if you're dating a Type One? Well, a good clue is if you happen to be Blossoms, my now-wife, and it's about five years ago. Back then

CLASSIC JAKE WISDOM

Beware of the Too-Casual Guy

 There are some men who have known nothing but casual relationships, and wouldn't know how to be intimate. If he doesn't even smile when you describe the cute thing you used to do with mashed potatoes when you were eight, you have one of these casual guys on your hands, and it's probably best to forget him.

-—JAKE, 1979

you (Blossoms) are getting mixed signals. Jake adores you: He loves your parents and your parents love him; he doesn't have any sort of a problem with intimacy or spending enormous amounts of time with you; you get no sense that he is leading or wants to lead a double life; you *know* he loves you. He's dedicated to you in every possible way—except the one way that matters most: He balks when it comes time to make a commitment. In your case, if you're Blossoms, getting engaged is the issue on the table, and for some reason he can't seem to discuss it without developing a slight stutter. You may also have noticed other symptoms; for example, that he's fixated on the idea of himself as a twenty-six-year-old with no responsibilities, even though he's not twenty-six anymore. Or that his eye wanders to women who aren't a real threat to you—women he'd clearly like to sleep with but nothing more. Not that that's not serious, but at least, you tell yourself, he's not looking to fall in love with someone else. He just seems to want to reserve a tiny sliver of himself to be free to do whatever it wants.

In short, if you feel like you have a guy who loves you—*really* loves you—but isn't committing fully to your relationship, then you've got a One on your hands. What should you do with him? It's probably the single most difficult question you'll face in your dating life, and I'm going to answer it for you: Give him a chance! Practice Jake's Rule #7 and give him (and a few other guys, simultaneously) a chance! At best, you'll have more men than you know what to do with. At worst, you'll have opened yourself up to the possibility that your One may not be *the one*, and you won't get the wind completely knocked out of your sails if things don't work out.

And now for the man we'll call Type Two. The Two is the guy we've been warning you about ("we" being your mother, your best friend and me). He's selfish, immature, possibly toxic and, for some reason, irresistible to you. While One is truly confused, Two is just pretending to be. He *knows* he won't commit and is not the least bit conflicted about it. It is Jake's belief that the Type Two will never fully turn himself around and be a good boyfriend, but Jake is wise enough to know that you need to figure this out for yourself. How can you do this? Broken-record time: by dating other guys.

Ever heard the saying about the frog and the pot? How if you put a frog in a pot of cold water and turn up the heat, the frog won't jump out of the pot, because he gets used to the heat going up incrementally? It's the same thing in a relationship—without a breath of fresh air from the outside, you might not realize yours is going stagnant or, worse, toxic. Take my friend Mike, who is a seemingly nice guy: sweet, funny, a laugh a minute. He loves dating, is quick to buy flowers or spring for a surprise trip to Miami for the weekend. But the thing about him is, that's as far as he wants to go. He's fun, but he's just not a boyfriend—he returns about half your calls, flakes out on half your plans, flirts with everyone. A *relationship* relationship just never ends up having much appeal to him. He'll keep being charming as long as you'll have him, which (he's charming, after all) is almost always too long for your own good. I remember one woman he dated who wouldn't stop seeing other people until she got a sign that he was a boyfriend type—and she never got it, so she ended up married to one of those other guys she was dating. And she told Mike, "The best way to realize you were not boyfriend material was for me to be around a guy who was."

Or consider the more toxic example of my friend Emily. When

she started dating Dan, he would always ask where she was going at night when he wasn't with her. This was a little annoying to her, sure, but she also thought it was sweet that he felt protective. Before long, though, he'd decided he didn't like some of her friends, and he asked her to skip hanging out with them. Then, shortly after Emily and Dan started lingering in front of jewelry store windows to compare notes on their favorite diamond settings, he decided he didn't like her going out without him at all. I remember her asking, "Do you think that's weird?" And I remember answering, "Um, yeah, it's psycho!"

But Emily was not ready to face the fact that Dan was wrong for her—and maybe actually wrong for *anybody*. She didn't believe it, truly believe it, until she met a guy named Eric in her tae kwon do class. They got to walking home from the studio together, and she soon found that Eric was the opposite of Dan: curious but not nosy, clearly interested in her but not obsessively so, laid-back instead of tightly wound. Eric was the breath of fresh air Emily needed to come to her senses and break up with control-freak Dan. The scary thing is, she might never have awoken from that trance had she never signed up, on a whim, for tae kwon do (following your whims—a good idea!).

Anyway, two years later, Emily is engaged to Eric. She's so happy—and relieved to have dodged the Dan bullet—that she tells all her friends in relationships to at least be *open* to other guys' interest in them; that being aware of who's out there can never hurt. "Dating Dan was like living in a police state!" she told me recently. "I can't *believe* I didn't see it until I met Eric."

In my experience, women lie to themselves about the nature

of the guys they're with for different reasons. Some, like Emily and Steph, do it because they're just steamrolled by their own romanticism. They want the boyfriend lifestyle and they want it now, and the idea of waiting around to find someone perfect is too maddening. Other women keep chasing men they know aren't good enough for them because they're afraid these guys are their last, best hope—because they're afraid of ending up alone. And others are so lacking in self-confidence that they don't even believe they deserve better; they end up dating a jerk, and that only makes them believe it's true that they don't deserve any better.

But you *do* deserve better—you do. If you want any power at all in your relationship, you have to start with that knowledge.

Women who lie to themselves about the quality of the guys they're with are afflicted with one of the gravest syndromes in the dating world. I call it "dating down." It's a condition I'm sad to say I learned a lot about from Jake readers. Every month when I was writing the column, I'd get letters like these:

From Lauren, in Virginia: "Do you think it's ever worthwhile to start something with a man who says he 'doesn't do relationships'? Is it possible he'll change his mind down the road? Or will you just feel horrible for starting it in the first place?"

From Yael, in California: "I need a shirt that says 'Jerk Magnet.' After beating myself up daily for the possibility that I did not put my all into my last failed relationship, I now realize that I was dating down. He was well aware of what I wanted from him and our relationship, and he chose never to deal with it."

From Rhianna, in Washington: "I was in a three-year relationship with a guy before I realized that it wasn't going to get any better. Of course, everyone around me already knew it but, try as they might, couldn't make me realize it. I finally opened my eyes and am now dating a wonderful man who treats me as if I'm the only woman on this earth."

The hardest thing about dating down is that it's a self-propelling vicious cycle. And I think one of the best ways to break that cycle is by, as Rule #7 states, keeping your options open. That way you're more likely to see that there are options, that there really *are* guys out there who aren't jerks. It's hard when you stop the cycle, because you feel like you've been wasting your time. But it's worth it. My old friend Steph isn't married with six kids as she once told me she wanted to be by the time she was thirty. But the good news is that she just dumped a real jerk, a bona fide Type Two. And it took her only about three weeks to do it instead of her usual six months. This time, she knew all the early warning signs by heart: He made big emotional promises right off the bat that he didn't keep; he blamed her discomfort in the relationship on her unreasonable demands; he never introduced her to his friends; and so on.

Not only has Steph dumped her latest downer, she's been on a few dates with a guy who seems like a definite boyfriend candidate. But to keep things from snowballing, Steph is still going on dates with other people. At least for now. She says it makes her feel like she has a little more control. I say she's finally tapping into her secret power. And like I said way back in the introduction to this book (don't you just love it when I quote myself?): Relationships aren't supposed to suck. You deserve to be loved; to be paid attention to; to gaze across the room, see your boyfriend and think,

God, am I lucky to be with that guy, and know he's thinking the same about you. The search for *that* guy might be frustrating and patience-testing and sometimes downright heartbreaking, but you will find him—and when you know in your gut that you have, the strongest thing you can do is to *stop* practicing Rule #7, and commit.

Four Signs It Might Be Time to Stop *Dating Other Guys*

So how do you know *when* to commit? Ideally, when you've checked off every one of these . . . and then given yourself another few weeks to think about it. Can't hurt.

You can have an argument without thinking, Well, *that* relationship was good while it lasted.

Everybody fights. Some very happy couples occasionally even slam doors or go to bed angry. The trick is doing it—and *not* seeing it as a sign of the apocalypse.

He leaves his email open.

Because he's got nothing to hide—and even though he'd be *annoyed* if you read it, he wouldn't be alarmed. (Still, try not to. That's basic respect for his privacy.)

There's photographic evidence.

Pictures of the two of you are all over his Facebook page, including a snapshot of you smooching at his birthday party. That's him letting the world—and any lurking exes—know you're serious.

"I" has become "We."

You barely noticed it at first, but then it was clear as day: "We can't make it." "We've got no plans this weekend." "Last night we made paella and watched the Michigan game." When even his most casual language slips into us-isms, he's in full-on couple mode.

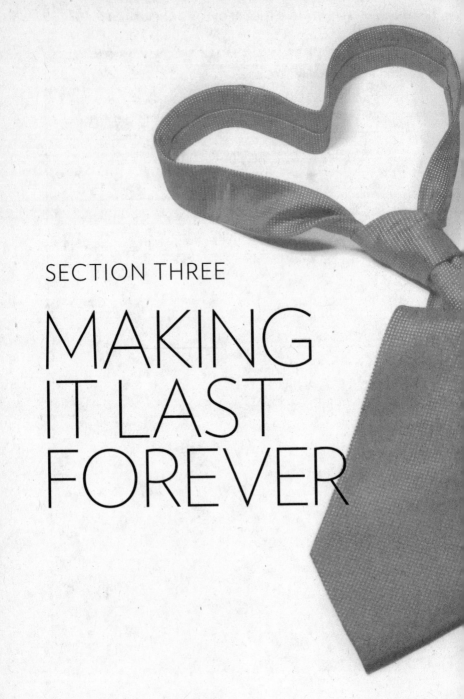

SECTION THREE

MAKING IT LAST FOREVER

So let's say you're monogamous, or close to it. You've followed Jake's Laws so far—you even kept dating other people far longer than you would have thought appropriate. But it worked and now you would like to go further. Marriage, maybe. Okay, marriage *definitely*. But—shocker—he's still a few steps behind you. So what will help him catch up? If he's capable—and most men are—*you* will. You're stronger than you've ever been. You've learned how to get inside the mind of your man and inspire the love you so totally deserve. Now you're ready to learn the Zen of Commitment: How to lead the man you love to it (without melodrama or ultimatums); how to be best friends but never just buddies; and how to enjoy the ride. It's all possible—if, yes, you use your secret power. Let's go!

Rule #8

Beware the Buddy Trap!

Or, a Woman of Intrigue Pees with the Door Closed

Not long ago, I met a few of my friends from college at a sports bar to watch our alma mater play football. We got a big table in front of a projection TV and ordered seventeen types of fried food, none of which actually tasted that good. We ate them in some sort of defiant act of manhood—*I swear I'm still the same dimwit I was in college!* All of us in the group were either married or in pretty serious relationships, which meant we felt extra pressure to "bro out" by drinking pitcher beer and trading intelligent observations about boobs. Immature, yes. But, ladies, don't diss Dudes' Night: It's good for you, too! Why? As 2010 Jake put it: "Like you, sometimes we need space. This has nothing to do with how we feel about you. It has to do with our need to preserve ourselves within a relationship. If you can be easygoing about this, we'll spend half our solo time thinking about how great you are—and then we won't need as much."

And so, for—I swear—the good of our relationships, my buddies and I talked about the women we slept with in college. We talked about the women we didn't sleep with in college but wanted to. The new fathers talked about how in love with their babies they were (hey, it's a fact—and we're modern and proud enough to express it). Eventually, we came to the part of the night—and it's part of almost every guys' night after age twenty-five—when we talked about the negotiations we'd made with our significant others in order to be there. Some of the guys said it was quid pro quo with their wives—to get approval for the guys' night, they'd preapproved a girls' night later on. One guy said he'd bribed his girlfriend by taking her out to a play and a fancy romantic dinner the week before. (This kind of thing depresses me to no end—the idea that romance is something you bribe women with and not something, you know, actually *romantic*.) I made everyone jealous by saying I hadn't had to negotiate with Blossoms at all (though I kept to myself the fact that she'd want to know every detail about my night the next morning). From there, of course, the talk turned to what the wives and girlfriends themselves were up to tonight. One guy's girlfriend was seeing some romantic comedy she knew he wouldn't want to see. Another's wife was eating pizza in bed— she loves reverting to her bachelorette days herself when she gets a chance. Some significant others were at home waiting for their dudes to come back after the game. One man said, with great weariness, that his wife couldn't fall asleep until he came home, so she was just sitting around waiting for him to return. That depressed *all* of us; nothing makes a night less enjoyable than knowing that the woman in your life is clocking you.

Then there was Joe. I don't know Joe well—he's a friend of a friend, and I see him only at these events. "Where's your wife, Joe?" someone asked. And he gave a pretty unexpected reply: "I have no idea."

Now, it's not the most insane thing I've ever heard, a guy not knowing where his wife is on any given night. It's not like we thought she'd left him for her goateed Pilates instructor. It's not like we thought she might actually be a CIA agent. But our interest, especially the interest of those among us who were married, was piqued. Joe's wife had suddenly become a woman of intrigue— and more so when Joe told us she wouldn't feel the need to share *everything* she'd done when they were apart. "Sometimes I think she goes to a café and reads a book," he told us. "Sometimes she goes salsa dancing, because I hate salsa dancing. Sometimes she just wanders around, sees a movie, sees friends. . . ." Joe went on to tell us that he didn't know if his wife would be sound asleep when he got home that night—or still out doing her thing. Didn't he worry? we wanted to know. "That's what texting is for," Joe said. "If I start to worry, I text her, and she answers right away. She's not sadistic, just independent!" And what about the recap? we asked. Would she expect a play-by-play the next morning of what *he'd* been up to? Joe shrugged again and smiled almost apologetically. "We might ask each other if it was a good night," he said, "and sometimes that leads to a pretty colorful conversation, but I've never once felt as if my wife was prying."

"Wow. This woman sounds hot," said the youngest guy in the group, a twenty-two-year-old from Joe's office.

"Oh, she is," said Joe, the smug bastard.

Mrs. Joe is a bit of a wonder. She's mysterious. And that's infinitely powerful. Before we get into how sexy a sense of mystery is, we need to talk about how important a *lack* of mystery is. It seems counterintuitive, but I believe a person has to be mostly a nonmystery before he or she earns the right to be mysterious. You have to tell your boyfriend or girlfriend where you are at night and during the day without them having to pry. You have to tell them when you're sick with the runs. You have to tell them that no one liked you in eighth grade and you ate your lunch in the computer lab to avoid admitting you had no friends in the cafeteria. Why? Because being in a *real* relationship means being able to tell your man friend or lady friend everything—not just the good stuff, or the stuff you think he or she wants to hear. As 2009 Jake put it: "Knowing and accepting each other? Being completely comfortable with your partner? I'm going to say nothing tops that for romance—except doing it all naked." And as my friend Dave once said to me, "I don't know what love is, but I know all I want in life is to be *completely* known by someone, and then completely loved by her. And for me to do the same with her." Awww, who wouldn't want that?

So in the beginning, if you truly care for this guy, let him see the real you: the you who's embarrassed about your knobby knees, and starts sweating profusely before meetings with your boss, and used to lie about your SAT score and took Prozac in college. Once you've shared all that, and he's let down his guard for you as well, congratulations, you're in a *real* relationship! And now—if you're anything like *Glamour* reader Crystal, from Indiana, who wrote to Jake, "How do you get the good stuff back? You know, the romantic stuff you did when you first started out?"—you probably need Rule #8.

Why is Rule #8 important? Because, as anyone who's been far enough down the relationship path knows, there is no finish line. Finding the right guy isn't like retiring: You never reach a point where you say, "Okay, I've worked hard to achieve the relationship I want, and now I can just kick back and enjoy it." You know in your gut that it doesn't work like that. Relationships evolve and grow and change just like you do. All of them require that you exercise your powers on a regular basis. Notice I didn't say, "A good relationship takes work," however. That expression is a pet peeve of mine, because it's rote and way too simple and, frankly, unsexy. What good relationships *do* take: surprises, left turns, moments of deeper understanding, a refusal to believe you've learned all the lessons. You and your hot-sex-and-deep-romance partner can't put your lives on cruise control once you find each other, or the sex will no longer be hot, and the romance will be nonexistent.

Keeping that romance going in a long-term relationship requires both parties to have, in a way, multiple personalities. You have to be able to be two different people to your significant other: the best friend and the sexy stranger. That's right, neither of you is doing the job if you're not both (1) the person most familiar to your mate, the person each of you is most comfortable around in the world; and, at the same time, (2) the person each of you is always wanting a little bit more of, who still possesses a touch of the foreign and the unfamiliar.

But please, get it out of your head that you have to *act* like two different people. You already *are* two different people. To paraphrase Walt Whitman, someone I have no right paraphrasing: You contain multitudes. Just as you contain both a proper lady who's offended by gratuitously disgusting jokes (and most of the *Jackass* movies) and a dirty-talking bedroom dynamo, you also contain the best friend and the sexy stranger. If you or your man have a hard time being either of these to each other, it's my prediction you're going to have trouble. If you're only the best friend, it could make for a sparkless relationship; if you're only the sexy stranger, neither of you will ever have a sense of stability and peace.

You know how some people say their relationships are in a rut? What they mean is that they're not being both of those people. More often than not, the sparkless rut comes from an overdevelopment of the roommate phenomenon: You're in a relationship for a while, you get comfortable. It's natural. It's good. But then you get too comfortable. You can't remember the last time you saw your man and he *wasn't* in flannel pajama bottoms. Maybe he stops wearing deodorant, or you make him buy your tampons all the time, and he makes you wash his underpants. You do everything together, everything, even stuff that requires a medical prescription or a bathroom stall. Not because it's fun—if you're both having fun, far be it from me to tell you to stop—but because it takes too much effort to do anything by yourself. And then you're dating your roommate. Your *brother*. The person you watch TV with until you go to bed. And you start to feel just the slightest bit unhappy in your love life. Here's how 2002 Jake put it:

Getting sucked into the Buddy Trap isn't anyone's "fault" per se, but men are more susceptible to its steely bite than women. In my experience, it's the guys who yearn for "someone I can just *relax* with." We're so accustomed to keeping our guard up—with women, with friends, with everyone—that after an exhausting sprint across the dating minefield, it's a huge relief to finally hunker down with someone we trust. Solid friendship is, of course, required. Without shared interests, meaty conversation and the ability to have fun together even while de-fleaing the dog, what do you have? Problem is, some of us men end up confusing romance with friendship, forgetting that couples need both. Eventually, we may not know whether to hug you or high-five you. The result: pals with nooky privileges. Not exactly the kind of relationship that's kept Hallmark in the black.

It happened to me and Blossoms. It's almost impossible for it *not* to happen. In fact, it's one bad symptom of a good relationship. But I remember one night when it really struck me. I was reading a book, already snacking in bed, with the Mets game on in the background. Blossoms slid into bed and started talking about how she'd been constipated because she was about to get her period. I had a little bit of a cold, so I blew my nose, hacked up a loogie (what, like you haven't had one?) and spit it into a Kleenex. Then Blossoms said, "Do you want to fool around?" What I should have said was "No! Let's build a moment of sexual tension here first! Let's have some romance! Let me at least brush the cookie crumbs off my pajama bottoms." But instead I said, "Sure, why not?" It was the least exciting sex I've ever had with Blossoms. It was to having sex what flipping around on the TV is to having a cultural experience: lame.

I credit Blossoms with saying afterward, "Things have to change."

It worked for us and it'll work for you: Start by closing the bathroom door. Listen, I'm not walking around with my head in the clouds. Of course, if you're going to be with someone for a long time, it's inevitable he's going to become familiar with all your bodily (and mental) functions. I'd even say you should fart in front of your guy, just once. Just so you have the monkey off your back. So you don't think that if you ever fart in front of the man you love, he'll think you're a gross human being. Do it. And then get past it. And then maybe refrain from doing it for another few years.

At this point in your relationship, I'm not advocating shame, or denial of humanity. What I'm advocating is putting a little effort into keeping your personhood separate from your man's. Just a little separation—a little breathing room to keep your personal business a bit personal.

Why does having space matter? Because space is power. The power to realize you don't *need* to do everything with him. The power to control your life instead of being part of a codependent pair; to choose to do things together rather than not knowing how to do them alone. Part of it has to do with realizing that your sexy instincts and your comfy instincts do not always work in tandem (though I'll admit that occasionally a comfy snuggle can turn into hot sex). Part of it is that absence, mystery, separateness—whatever

CLASSIC JAKE WISDOM

"I *Don't* Want My Mommy!"

> Of course, as a relationship progresses, we men expect more PDA (pathetic-date-assistance). Showing up with a new shower curtain is fine if, say, you do a lot of bathing at our place and don't like mildew. But rearrange our furniture, provide us with a drawerful of miraculously clean socks and hand over a new Dustbuster "just because," and suddenly we're back to Mom forcing us into a sailor suit for the annual portrait sitting at Sears. Bottom line: Guys are grateful for caring gestures, but we can't stomach obvious spoon-feeding.
>
> —JAKE, 2001

you call it—creates the possibility of fantasy and a little healthy objectification. And, partly, you need that breathing room because of what Joe and his wife (remember them from the beginning of the chapter?) were doing right. Because she established a little bit of space, she got him wondering about her, talking about her, even bragging about how sexy she is in the middle of a sports bar. And instead of feeling like he had to carve out his own space, he was free to imagine her in hers. She, as I said earlier, gave him the room to pursue her a little bit. She gave him the space to *desire*.

I'm not just talking about literal space. I'm talking about keeping part of you for *you*. I'm talking about feeling independent and being just 1 percent mysterious; about putting up at least a few little barriers to being 100 percent known. I'm talking about not intermingling your lives so extremely that you stop being your own person—no matter how long you've been dating or married. There's little that's sexier to a guy, after all, than your independent streak (see Rule #1). It can be hard to keep that streak streaking—it can feel much easier just to sink into the total comfort of a long-term relationship. But use your power and resist! I'm talking about not talking on the phone every thirty seconds all day, keeping each other abreast of even the most mind-numbing minutiae. I'm talking about taking up a hobby that has nothing to do with him. I'm talking about getting a radical haircut without consulting him first.

And now, back to that bathroom door. There's nothing patently wrong with keeping it open. And hey, you might be able to have a long, happy, intriguing and mysterious relationship and still pee in plain view of each other. Besides, there are plenty of sexy things you do in the bathroom; no guy minds seeing you leaning over the bathroom sink in your bra and panties, applying mascara; or naked and wrapping your hair in a towel—that's pretty hot too. But we don't need to see (or hear) *everything*. We'll love you just as much, of course, but it may, just may, reduce the . . . mystery. Men are fantasy addicts, just like you. When we lie in bed on business trips, thinking of you, we don't want to think of you tweezing your ingrown bikini hairs.

But, like I said, being mysterious isn't just about what you *don't* do in front of your partner. It's about what you *do* do as well! Here are a few more ways to exercise your feminine powers once you've found a man you love:

1) Be a stranger once in a while. Dress differently when you go meet him. Sing along to an album you love that he's never heard before. Sounds cliché, but pretend to be a stranger in a bar and pick him up. Blossoms did this with me once, and I can tell you, the man who gets to have an affair with his own wife is a lucky man indeed.

2) If you're a bit of an exhibitionist, don't walk around naked *all* the time. Remember how exciting it was in the beginning, when you weren't quite comfortable with each other, and then suddenly someone walked across the room wearing nothing but a smile? That's a sexy moment, and you can't relive it if you make a habit of going over the grocery list or talking to your credit card company in your birthday suit. That said . . .

3) If you're the modest type who wears a tracksuit to bed, let him watch you strut around the house in your birthday suit just once a week. See Rule #2: "Know How Sexy You Really Are."

4) Make a new friend. You're an interesting woman. You like to explore, seek out new ground. And if your guy is as awesome as you are, he'll think that's pretty damn hot of you; men find it sexy when women stake their own claim in the world. A healthy way to expand your horizons when you're in a relationship is to make a new friend now and again. Female, male, who cares—just forge a connection with someone from outside your social circle. Forget about what it does for him—do it for yourself.

5) Take some time for yourself, and don't share everything you did unless he specifically asks. That's Joe's wife's secret. I think it's a good one. He loves getting to try to pry info out of her rather than have it foisted on him. And she feels more independent, which makes her feel more powerful, which . . . you should know what that means by now.

Your next objective here—something a lot of women I've talked to have a hard time with—is to let *him* be a little mysterious too. There's a certain conversation that almost all my guy friends have had with their girlfriends or wives at least once, and it's a conversation that sucks. It goes like this:

> HER: What did you do last night?
> HIM: Had dinner with Josh.
> HER: What did you talk about?
> HIM: I don't know. Work, women, the Mets.
> HER: What about work?

Him: I don't know. Just what's going on at his office.

Her: What *is* going on at his office?

Him: I don't remember! I'm sorry.

I'm terrible at re-creating conversations.

Her: Okay.

Him: Netflix came. Should we make popcorn and
watch the movie?

Her: So you talked about women?

You pump us for information because you're interested in our lives, in our evenings, in our conversations, because the jealous part of you wants to make sure we have our stories straight. But no guy likes to be interrogated. Especially about his solo time. And hey, I get it, you ask all those questions only because your guy would never tell you *anything* if you didn't pry it out of him. You hate having to grill us, but we suck at communicating, so what else are you supposed to do?

That's a damn good question. The answer is to hold back a little and let him come to you with the information. I can also tell you that when you ask us a million questions about what we've been up to without you, it makes us feel as if you don't trust us. And if you actually *don't* trust your guy after, say, six months, you probably never will and should ask yourself why. But if that's not the case, get comfortable with the idea that you don't need to know *everything* your partner does. In fact, the less you indulge that need to follow his every move, the more powerful you'll feel, no doubt about it. Early on in our relationship, Blossoms, having gone through some jealous phases in her life, for a time wanted to know the verbatim transcript of every conversation I had with another woman. What did we talk about and did she flirt and did I flirt, and so on. It got to the point where I actually felt like I was lying even when I wasn't. But after we broke up and got back together— after she went through a period where she found her power— she hardly ever asked me more than a passing question about my lunches and meetings with other people, women included. That made me more comfortable sharing all that stuff with her. And she found she felt much better about herself.

Now, dear readers, I want you to do something for yourself: Ask your guy to read this chapter too. Maybe it'll stir something in him the next time he's about to leave his toenail clippings on the toilet seat; or before he decides to cool down from his workout in his sweaty gym shorts on your couch; or when he's tempted to seduce you with lines like, "C'mon baby, just pull my finger." (C'mon yourself, man, if you're reading this!) If nothing else, you'll feel empowered from having tried.

The Three Laws of Living Together

Should you move in with him? And what will it do to your love and sex life? 2008 Jake had some advice.

1 **If you don't know his middle name, you're definitely not ready.** My experiment in cohabitation began like a dream. I met a gorgeous woman, told her I loved her within a week and moved in on our one-month anniversary. Our first night as roomies, we ordered Chinese and watched nine minutes of *Meet the Parents* before making love on the couch for three hours. I moved out four months later with my belongings in a Hefty bag. What doomed us? Well, mostly it was 1,001 little daily annoyances. What I learned is that you need to take the time to discover a person's good quirks so their *bad* quirks are worth tolerating. If she had known me long enough to learn my middle name, I'd have had the chance to prove how unflaggingly loyal I can be, and she might have forgiven me for using a fork as a back scratcher.

2 **It's still okay to be independent.** Why? Because you're still different people. My friends Dana and Carl don't even eat dinner together. As soon as Dana comes home, she orders Thai or Indian food for herself; later on, Carl eats, in his words, "something beige."

"I like it early and spicy, Carl likes it late and plain," jokes Dana. "Except when it comes to, ahem, dessert."

3 **Try exchanging keys first.** My friends Matt and Amy have discovered the cohabitation middle ground; they each made the other a set of keys to their separate homes. "Now she's got my whole top drawer for her stuff, but we still have our own spaces," Matt says. "It's like she's moving in, one sock at a time."

As for me, I think I'm going to go old school and wait until I'm married before I live with another woman. In the meantime, I'm working on that back-scratching thing.

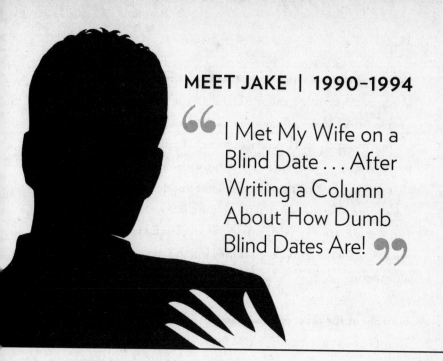

MEET JAKE | 1990–1994

66 I Met My Wife on a Blind Date... After Writing a Column About How Dumb Blind Dates Are! 99

Early-nineties Jake, like several others over the years, used the column to chronicle his journey from Hapless Single Guy to Madly-in-Love Grown-up. His guts-and-all honest takes on being in a long-distance relationship (including how guys get over the urge to cheat) had readers rooting for the romance to succeed. It did: Jake and the woman he code-named "A." are happily married to this day. Later, he wrote a novel about the experience, Now I Know Everything.

What was the best part about writing the Jake column?
Being able to say honestly—with complete immunity and impunity—exactly what I wanted to say about romance, dating and sex. The pseudonymity of Jake released me from any sort of timidity.

What was the most important thing you wrote as Jake?

I remember writing a column about all the (phony) reasons men give to break up or pull away—and the fact is, most of it is face-saving, cowardly stuff. A female friend of mine, who was in a tortured on-again, off-again relationship with a guy, thanked me after that column and said she'd always known, deep down, that what I'd written was true, but that the column was refreshing and helpful. Women wrote in fairly often to thank me for saying what they trusted to be the truth, even if they weren't happy about it in the short term.

How about the most controversial?

I wrote one about date rape that generated a flurry of letters—I'd say they ran about even for supporting what I said and slamming it. The point I made was this: I said that if you have trouble holding your liquor, sorry, but you should drink less when you're out at a bar or club. Those who hated me for saying it said I was perpetuating the old, awful, misogynistic stereotype that women who get into trouble somehow asked for it. But my point was that there are assholes out there. And two drunk, impaired people are more trouble than one. I still think it's true.

Did you end up finding your true love?

Yes, I did. I met Alex about a year into my stint. I fell in love at first sight and started writing about the relationship (referring to her as "A."). We've been together almost twenty years. Married for sixteen. We have three kids. I'm still nuts about her, even more so.

We met on a blind date. Not long before that I had written a column about how truly worthless and dumb blind dates were. (I'd been on a few before, and they had yielded nothing, and the artifice and uncomfortableness had turned me off.) But 1.3 seconds into that blind date with A., I knew I would need to write a follow-up column on how profoundly wrong I had been about blind dates.

Make Him Think Commitment Was His Idea

How to Lead Your Guy to the Big C
So Gently, He Won't Even Know
He's Being Led

You're going to accuse me of generalizing about men. And you'll have a point—all men are different. Some men want nothing more than to rent movies and snuggle every night, and others would rather cut off their own hand with a spork than do that. There are men who require some solitude and others who can't stand to be alone for five minutes. There are even those among us who don't like porn or who have no trouble crying. Not only that, but men don't want to be generalized—we don't like thinking we're interchangeable. We're individuals!

Okay. Now that I've cleared that up, I can get to my general(ized) point: Men don't care about commitment.

Maybe that's going a little too far. Let's just say that the average man doesn't care about commitment *as much* as the average woman does. It's not that he's terrified: The typical man doesn't actually get the sensation that he's being buried alive when he thinks about committing. In fact, the vast majority of the men out there probably think pretty positively about long-term relationships, marriage, children and all the rest. But still, there's a not-so-subtle inequality in *how much* we desire these things as compared to you.

Maybe this is the best way to explain it: Men may like the idea of commitment, they just don't feel like they *need* it. In order to get this chapter right, I talked to a bunch of my friends—male and female—about the big C. What they thought about it, how they felt about it, how badly they yearned for it. My friend Tara had what I think is the most interesting answer of all the women I talked to. She taught me a lot. Here's what she said:

You know the way a lot of men feel about sex? That they kind of have to have it or they're going to go nuts? That they may sometimes find themselves wanting it from anyone, appropriate or not? That's how I feel about commitment. I have a kind of animalistic need. A nameless urge in my chest that can only be satisfied by feeling like I'm about to move into a three-bedroom starter house to make some children. Sometimes when I feel that animalistic need, it doesn't even have to do with the guy, and that's when I really get myself into trouble. And when I get the sense I'm not going to get it, I get desperate. It's not that I haven't known my share of guys who are desperate to commit, but in my experience, it's different. Most men who feel that need—it's usually about a specific woman. But for a woman, it has to do with that urge. Like I said, it's like the opposite of how gender roles work when it comes to sex: We both want it, but in this case, it's women who are a little out of control.

Who knows why women's urges for commitment sometimes feel more primal than men's? You could definitely argue that it's socialized—I know a lot of women who feel judged about when and if they get married or have kids. Or you could argue that it's pure biology: The need to have a family and to nest may be the female counterpart to that famous male need to spread his seed. But I'm not a sociologist or an evolutionary biologist. I'm just a guy who's struggled with commitment issues himself and, through those struggles, figured out something important. This is how men exert power over you in a relationship: by not caring as much about commitment and marriage as you do. *This is our only advantage!* When a man doesn't care as much as his girlfriend does about being exclusive, getting engaged, moving in, having a baby, having another baby or whatever form of commitment is getting you all hot under the collar, the ball is firmly in his court. *He* gets to decide when and whether these things will happen. And he doesn't respond very well to being pushed into a decision by his better half.

"Gee, thanks, Jake!" you're probably saying. "What am I supposed to do with this information?" Well, first you should keep practicing Rule #7: Keep Dating Other People Longer Than You

Think You Should. And second, you should let him think commitment was *his* idea. That's how you'll get the ball back into your court. And you know how much you like to hold that ball.

First, Avoid the Standoff

Okay, let me tell you a story about a friend of a friend of mine, Michael. Michael had been dating Christine for about three years. She wanted them to move in together, which she saw as being "engaged to be engaged." That's how she explained it to all her friends. "I don't need to be married right this second," she said. "I just need to feel like I'm on the path and I'm not wasting my time here." For a while, she said this stuff only to her friends and not to Michael himself. Not that he didn't know it. If you're in a relationship for three years and you don't know that your girlfriend wants to be engaged to be engaged—which more often than not really just means she'd like to get married—then you are not a very perceptive guy. But as Michael hadn't responded to her hints that they should move in together, let alone start looking for an accent color and bridesmaids' dresses, she decided she was going to lay down the law with him. She figured she was being powerful by making her needs known. Fair enough; you can respect her for standing up for herself. But once she started talking about it, it started to dominate their relationship. Over and over again, she demanded that he explain why he didn't want to commit. And the more she asked, the less he was able to explain himself. He fumbled his words, feeling exceedingly guilty, and said he didn't want to talk about it. And that only made things worse.

What did Michael do in the face of all this pressure? He dug in his heels. My buddy Art has a saying: Men like commitment *in the abstract*. It's when it becomes real that we get a little freaked out. And Michael's version of getting freaked out was to become totally confused. "I have no idea what *I* want," he told our mutual friend, "because all I can think about is what *she* wants. Because she puts it in my face all the time."

He thought everything would be fine if Christine would just stop talking about *it* long enough for him to figure out what he wanted. But by that time, they were in a kind of standoff. He was waiting for her to leave him alone so he could feel like he was making his own decision; she was waiting for him to finally *say something*. They both felt the other person was totally not understanding them. They both felt like the aggrieved party. They started fighting more. And every fight they had ended up being the exact same fight: Why couldn't he commit? They became one of those nightmare couples you never want to go out to dinner with—the tension was always high, the threat of a blowup always there.

Eventually, Christine did it. She gave him the ultimatum. She said: "Either you move in with me or we break up." She'd been driven almost insane by his half responses. And Michael had been driven almost insane by her incessant pressure. It seemed to him like the only honest thing to do was to "take a break" from the relationship. So he said, "I knew this was coming, and I can't say that I blame you. But I can't hear myself think. I don't even know what I want. I need some time." And she said, "You know what, Michael? You can have all the time you need. You can have all the time in the world. I'm not waiting to hear what you've thought about. This is goodbye."

And that was it. That *was* goodbye. Which is awfully, terribly sad—and, if you ask me, avoidable.

Listen, I know we men are really frustrating when it comes to this stuff. I know it would seem like we need nothing more than a push. I know that telling us we need to commit feels like a way of seizing your power, which is what this whole book is all about. But once that becomes topic A of the relationship, it can make your man feel powerless, which is a feeling he'll go to the ends of the earth to avoid. Men want to be the masters of our own destinies, even though as often as not we'd be totally lost without you and barely able to decide what to buy at the supermarket. This is one of the most important decisions we'll ever make, and we want to feel as if we're making it on our own.

So if you push, if you firmly issue an ultimatum, you may well not get the result you were hoping for. The relationship may change on you. You may find yourself in a Michael and Christine situation. Consider yourself warned.

Second, Lead Him to the Water— Then Step Back

Okay, great, Jake, you're thinking. So if we stand up for what we really need in a relationship, we're poisoning the well. Why not just tell us we shouldn't bother dating men?

Well, as a man, sometimes I would like to tell you to stop dating men. I wouldn't have wanted to date me during many periods of my life, and I can't think of a single one of my guy friends who'd be a cakewalk either. But if you're not into dating women or having a super-deep relationship with Netflix, we're kind of the only game in town. So you're left with us, many of whom would never get married if you waited for us to make the decision—not because we're against it or don't want to be with you or anything, but just because, as we have been discussing, it never felt that pressing.

The only thing to do if you find yourself in a situation like Michael and Christine's—where your man reminds you of nothing so much as a really stubborn donkey who will not be pulled forward—is to help him come to the decision that it's time to commit *entirely on his own* (wink, nudge). Some would say this is manipulative, and I'd say . . . well, I guess that's true. But I prefer to see it as you leading us toward what we really want to do anyway. (Because it *is* what we want anyway! More on that a little later.)

How do you lead a man to make this decision on his own? Delicately, compassionately, lovingly. We *are* talking about someone you love, after all. So below are six ways to go about getting him to believe that commitment is coming from his corner and not yours. You can pick and choose the ones that work for you—one approach may do it, or a combination of several might be your best fit. You'll know.

Commitment approach #1: Never bring it up. I mean never. This is a pretty radical technique, but it worked for my friend Nancy. She wanted to marry her (now) husband about three minutes after she met him. She didn't exactly say this out loud, because she understood it was a little crazy. Because she knew she should get to know him a little better before deciding to spend the rest of her life with him. And because she's a perceptive woman, and she sensed that this was a guy who really cherished his independence.

He was in a band (red flag) and he ran marathons, plus lots of other stuff that indicated his need for solitude and self-reliance. So she decided never, ever to bring up commitment. And it was hard, because he didn't bring it up for a long time either. Meanwhile, she didn't hide her feelings for him; I would never advise anyone to do that. One of the best moments in any relationship, as I said in the last chapter, is when you take the risk and tell the other person how you feel. Nancy told her boyfriend how she felt *about him* all the time—she was crazy about him, loved his body, couldn't wait to see him after work most evenings . . . but she never mentioned the idea of moving in. She never asked him how old he wanted to be when he got married (she knew he didn't think in those terms). In fact, she talked about it so little that eventually— she says it was about eight months into the relationship—he started wondering if he was the only one who wanted to take things to, as he called it, the next level. To which she said, "Why, actually, I've been thinking about it all along." Now, by no means is this something every woman should try, or something that's a good idea with every guy. You don't want to feel like you're being dishonest all the time, and you don't want to feel like you're spending a good chunk of your brainpower muzzling yourself. This is a special prescription for women who either (a) feel they jump the gun on bringing up commitment or (b) get the distinct impression that while the guy they're with loves them, he needs to feel that commitment was *his* idea.

Commitment approach #2: Go on with your life, without being a martyr about it. This is what Blossoms did, if you remember. She wanted to live in a new apartment, she'd been saving up for it, and

How to Talk to a Man About Your Future

" Given that there are at least two surefire ways to freak out a man who likes you a lot—talking explicitly about the future ("I can't wait until our grandson asks to borrow the car") or disavowing any chance for a mutual future ("Staying up all night with the other nuns talking about God will be wonderful")—you may be wondering what legitimate options are available to you for discussing events beyond next weekend.

Be light. Whenever possible, be unspecific. Whenever you feel like bringing up the future, wait a day, then wait another week, and *then* bring it up.

Even if you're with a guy you feel understands you, a guy with whom you're totally open, don't discuss—not for a good long time, anyway—wedding bands (the gold or the four-piece kind), what city you'd like to live in, whether the house will be aluminum-sided or not. We men are not deaf and we're not slime, but, I hate to admit it, we always have to believe we're in total control of our destinies. And the only way we're going to believe that is if we get to come to you one day and ask what exactly you had in mind now that we've been together a happy while.

—JAKE, 1993 "

so she decided she was going to buy it. She didn't use it as an ultimatum—she never said, "Either move in with me or I'm going to get my own apartment." She was really cool about it and even asked me to help her look for it. She gave me the space I needed to pursue her. And it totally worked. I didn't want her buying an apartment without me, considering I wanted to spend the rest of my life with her!

Commitment approach #3: Suggest it without suggesting it. I don't mean saying things like, "I don't know why I'm asking, but I was just thinking, would you rather have a big wedding or a small wedding, whenever it is you get married and, you know, whoever it is you get married to?" Most men will see that as crossing the line into straight-up passive-aggressive behavior—which it is. What I'm suggesting you try here is more like what my friend Alexis did to her boyfriend, Tommy. First, she had a talk with him. She said, "I just want to make sure you're comfortable with where our relationship is." That got him thinking about where exactly their relationship was, which was, honestly, kind of stalled. Then she got him to talk about what his life goals were, and when he wanted to make those goals happen. If a man has a goal of having a wife and kids, setting out a timeline can help him realize he'd better get going. And if that's not his goal, isn't it better to know right away? Then she asked what she could do to help him achieve his goals. In Tommy's case, he wanted to go to business school. That was part of the reason he felt like he couldn't settle down—he didn't feel like he was living his life yet. So she signed him up for the GMAT. And then he asked her to help him study, so she did. And once he was accepted to school, suddenly he felt a tremendous need to get

Alexis to settle down with him. She had helped him realize that if you don't go after what you want, life just passes you by.

Commitment approach #4: Take on the role of the person who's wary of commitment. Sometimes when one party in a relationship is going one hundred miles an hour, the other party feels she or he needs to put on the brakes. So if you know you're prone to being the hundred-mile-an-hour person, try turning the tables. Say something like, "I am so totally into you, but I'm not even going to think about moving in with you for a long time to come. I have a habit of rushing into things, but I am learning to prioritize my independence." See, you've simultaneously planted a seed (moving in together) and removed any sense of urgency about it. The idea is to make him the one trying to convince *you* to go faster. Now, it's never a good idea to lie about how you feel—not very powerful. But if you tell him that, in the past, you've gone for commitment at warp speed, and you're at a phase in your life where you want to slow it down—and that's really how you feel? That seems pretty honest to me.

Commitment approach #5: Help him make the decision without making the decision. I've got a lot of friends who've ended up being in committed relationships this way. Here's how it goes. First his toothbrush comes over. Then some underwear. His apartment sucks anyway; it's always messy, there's never any food and he has that noisy upstairs neighbor, so you encourage him to spend more and more time at your place. You ask if he wouldn't mind chipping in for groceries since he eats them all anyway—maybe even for the electricity bill since he insists on keeping the AC on all the time despite the fact that it's killing the polar bears. And, eventually, you're living together. Now, here's the crucial part, the part that makes this approach work: You wonder aloud whether this isn't *too* comfortable. "Doesn't it almost feel like we're living together?" You tell him that if you decide to live together, it shouldn't be by default, even though you love it. And then maybe you suggest that he spend a little more time at his place. And after spending a little more time at his place and realizing that it sucks compared to spending time with you, he says (if he's like my friend Eric): "I want to move in with you." Because he's figured out through experience that living with you trumps living by himself or with his slobby roommate. He's tasted life with you, but without you standing over his shoulder saying, "Taste it! It's wonderful!"

Commitment approach #6: When the moment of truth comes, don't flinch. There comes a time when you need to admit to yourself you've waited as long as you want to wait, and that you want commitment or you want nothing. If you've tried some, or all, of the above tactics and the man you want to marry doesn't seem to want to marry you, then it's time to say it straight-out. How do you do that? Well, you need to have compassion for your man, and you need to be kind. You may end up remembering this moment for the rest of your life. But you also need to be entirely clear. A good way to say it might be: "I love you, and I want to make a life with you. But I also realize that timing isn't always perfect. And if you're not ready to take the plunge, that's okay. But I'm going to need to start over with someone else." This is a power move, remember. It's not pathetic in the slightest. Your man is going to feel much more pathetic—because he'll know that not being able to decide always feels weaker than knowing what you want. I probably don't have to tell you this, but it's worse to cling to a relationship that's making you miserable than it is to ask for what you want and know that you may end up with nothing. (Nothing from him, anyway; but you'll end up with closure, and that's something.) So fess up when you know that waiting another minute would be disrespecting yourself, and know that you deserve to have the relationship you want.

So you've gotten this far in the chapter, but there's something that's unsettling you. Bravo. That discomfort means you're a good human being. Because if you're at all a nice person, you don't welcome the idea of manipulating your boyfriend, crush, husband—or, really, anyone else. And I have to say that, by and large, I agree with that. Honesty kind of beats out everything else when it comes to worthwhile tactics. But I'm going to help you rationalize here: When it comes to commitment, you should realize that by manipulating us, you're actually helping us.

First of all, a good guy doesn't *want* to hold all the power in a relationship—not the kind of power that comes with constantly disappointing the person you love. It's not a fun power to have, take it from me. And for this guy at least, there's no better feeling in the world than giving up that power. Plus, even though men are aware of the cliché about us being commitment-phobes, those of us who embody that cliché don't feel normal. I say this from experience. We look around and see all our happily committed friends and family members and think, *What's wrong with me?*

Second, remember that, as my friend Art noted, most men

really do like commitment *in the abstract*. When we imagine our best selves, our best futures, it's almost always a future centered around a committed relationship. Making the decision, in real life, to effectively murder your former self (this is how commitment-phobes see it) can feel extremely hard. But we want to get from abstract commitment into real-life commitment. And if we realize that we are being manipulated a tiny bit, or at least being left alone for longer than is optimal for the woman in our life—well, if it gets us where we secretly want to go, we're often relieved. I know a ton of guys who claim to have gone kicking and screaming into commitment, while simultaneously being grateful they were dragged into adulthood.

One very important note: Before you run out and try Rule #9 on the man in your life, I advise you to take a cold, hard look at *why* he's not committing. A lot of men are scared to commit even to the women they really love—these are the men on whom this law can work wonders. But there are also men, not to mention women, who don't commit because they don't want to be with the person they're with, and they're blaming it on the general problem of commitment phobia because it's easier than saying the truth. These men are in what I call zombie relationships. Neither dead nor alive, they merely lurch unhappily through the countryside, you know, marauding and stuff. Man, I have been in a couple of these, and they're miserable. I remember actually telling one girlfriend that I was afraid of commitment (when really I just couldn't stomach the confrontation), because I knew it was a cliché and she'd be likely to believe me. Cowardly. And all too common.

So be careful that you're not wasting all your powers of persuasion on a zombie. If you're not sure whether you're in a zombie relationship, just ask yourself: Is this guy not really into being with me? Do I get the sense that he's waiting around for something better? Do I get the vibe that he'd like a rock to fall on him to get him out of this predicament? Does he have that same forlorn look about him as a person in a bus station at 2 a.m.? If you answer yes to any of those questions, run. Do not go back for your toothbrush. Do not wait for him to end it himself. Just follow this still-fresh advice from 1966 Jake: "Baby, don't get sidetracked. Cut this fellow off now. You're rationalizing, and making up excuses for him, and hoping that he'll turn out to be the real thing, largely because there's no real thing on the horizon, right now, to engage your attention. But when it comes along—and it will—you'll know it."

Five Ways to Drive Him Crazy (the Bad Way) About Commitment

've told you everything I know about how to lead a man gently into the committed relationship of your dreams. Now for five things it's really important *not* to do:

Publicly tease him about his commitment phobia

It's never a good idea to shame your significant other in public about his breath, about his too-long stories and, most especially, about committing to you. It makes him feel awful, it makes you look mean, and it airs dirty laundry that should be kept to intimate conversations between you and your best friend.

Assume he's going to pop the question at every major holiday

Why did my now-wife, Blossoms, think I was going to propose over our first Christmas? I hate Christmas! I can't tell you how many guys I know who have come back from some big event—the first-time visit with a girlfriend's family, a tropical vacation, even a high school reunion—and reported that their girlfriend had started crying and/or screaming because she'd imagined he was going to propose. It makes us fear holidays! And it keeps us from buying you any jewelry in a little box lest you think it's a ring.

Constantly talk about how all your friends are getting married

Listen, it's totally understandable if you feel a tad competitive. But no one wants to get married because his girlfriend's best friend from college just got married. It's a losing argument.

Give an ultimatum more than once

If you're going to say something like, "If we're not living together by my thirtieth birthday, I'm walking" (which, in Jake's opinion, is courting disaster), you need not fear that he'll forget it. Once really is enough. And sorry, but if you lay down an ultimatum like that, for your sake, you've gotta follow through. If he lets you walk away and it's truly a relationship that's meant to last, he'll come knocking.

Talk and talk about your biological clock

The biological clock is a real thing. It very well might be at the root of womankind's collective burning need for commitment. But once you've established that your clock is ticking, don't keep reminding your boyfriend about it. When you say you have only a certain number of years left to have a baby, he *knows* that you really mean that you have only a certain number of years left to meet his mother, plan a wedding, vacation somewhere exotic, buy a starter home, stock a freezer and start procreating. Yes, he knows all that. Making him feel like a schmuck is not the answer. What is? Reread this chapter already!

Rule #10

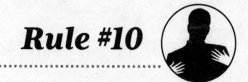

And Above All, Enjoy the Ride!

Because Love Is Meant to Be Fun—
and Women Who Know That Are the
Most Powerful Women of All

know I've been telling you to follow rules; to put some effort into dating instead of just unconsciously making the same mistakes over and over again; to go out and kick ass as a woman. I believe all that stuff or I wouldn't have said it. But it's also important to realize this isn't *work*. This isn't a matter of national security. This stuff is supposed to be fun. In fact, it's basically the most fun thing in the entire experience of being human.

I'll never forget one of the last dates I went on before I met Blossoms. It was a setup—my friend Eric worked with my date, Suz, at his sports marketing company, and he told me she was the only person he knew who was as sarcastic as I was. I came straight from the gym to our date, trudging into the bar with wet hair, my workbag across one shoulder and my gym bag across the other. I was feeling harried, weighed down and ready to have a giant beer. Suz was waiting for me, and I got pretty excited once I saw her. She was tall, in a tight blouse that was somehow both businessy and sexy, with long brown hair restrained in the back by some kind of comb. She had an assertive presence, if that makes any sense: a confident look in her eyes, upright bearing—she looked like the kind of woman who knows she could ace you in tennis.

So I ordered myself that big beer. She had a vodka soda. I gulped down about half my drink in less than two seconds and was feeling pretty good. It was one of those moments when everything hits you perfectly: a little buzz, a little postworkout high, that initial hopefulness of meeting another person (who is attractive) when it seems like anything is possible. It was shaping up to be the best blind date I'd been on in a long, long time. Suz was as sarcastic as advertised. As we bantered flirtatiously for a while, she had a way of saying almost everything so that it came across as a challenge. Like when she said, "So you're coming from the gym?" as if I were lying about it, or as if I were some dumb jock. Or "You drank that beer pretty quickly," as if she suspected that I was unable to drink beer any other way. Or "You're a writer," as if she were really saying, "I know what writers are all about—you're all up to no good." At first I liked the way she seemed to be baiting me; she was clearly a strong woman, but her tone was sweetly tough, not steely. Little did I know, though, that this was about to change big-time.

Soon we were playing a drinking game where we'd go back and forth naming state capitals until one of us got one wrong—and the loser would have to buy the next round.

"Pierre, South Dakota!" I said.

"Columbus, Ohio," she countered. "And their state bird is the cardinal!"

We continued like that for a while, each trying to out-nerd the other with our U.S. of A. trivia. I made what I thought was a mildly flirty, and honest, comment that this was one of the best dates I'd been on in a long time, even though it had been only twenty minutes. The look on her face changed. She rolled her eyes like, "Yeah, I wonder how many times you've said that this week." Her mood totally shifted.

"Jake," she said, though obviously she didn't use the name Jake, "I've asked around about you. I know about your history. I know about you, and I know about guys like you. You're charming. You like to date. You like to audition as the perfect boyfriend even though you've got no intention of being anyone's boyfriend for long. You think you're not a player because you know what the state capital of South Dakota is, but you're still a player. And I want you to know I know better. I've been around the block a few times, and I'm not playing any games. So let's cut the crap. I'm not going to be charmed by you that easily—you're going to have to go a long way toward proving you're serious."

The night, as you might imagine, came to a screeching halt. The new-chemistry euphoria wore off. The rest of the date proceeded like a strained meeting between exes. Civil, I guess, but that's about it. I was attracted to her, but I was freaked out. I was afraid to flirt with her because I was sure that would somehow make me guilty of being the jerk she thought I was. We finished our drinks. I steered the conversation toward the most respectful, nonplayer topics I could think of—work, travel, parents—and then we ended up talking about, I kid you not, her accountant. We never saw each other again.

I know this sounds mean, but Suz ruined our date. She sabotaged it in the same way that many, many women do—by expecting the worst from men, by walking into a new relationship with defenses up and fists bared instead of treating us like individuals worth getting to know. She thought she was being powerful, but she was really just protecting herself in a way that was self-sabotaging. Now, was she *wrong* about my flaws? Not really: I do like to flirt with women—and back then, I *really* liked to flirt with women. I was also, in those pre-Blossoms days, guilty of having failed at a bunch of relationships. But contrary to Suz's accusations on our date, I've never flirted with the intention of taking advantage of the woman. On the contrary, the best part about every one of my flirtations leading up to Blossoms was the chance that this was going to turn out to be some formative moment, a sea-changing event, the beginning of *the rest of my life.*

For most of us, dating is a journey to that moment. You can be like Suz and look wearily at that journey, see it as something to fight your way through, or you can trust that each of these encounters has the capacity to be truly exciting and interesting and fun for what it is. You can go along with the dating train and see where it takes you. In other words—here it comes—you can *enjoy* the ride.

So Dust That Chip Right Off Your Shoulder

Maybe you've found the right guy, the one you want to keep around for a while; if that's the case, awesome! You should feel free to skip ahead to the next section: Why We Should All Be a Little Bit More French. But maybe you're still looking. Maybe you've been on a million dates. Maybe you've given your number out at football games and Laundromats, collected numbers at what feels like a hundred parties. Maybe you've been poked on Facebook more times than a person should be poked by anyone other than her doctor. And you're tired. I get it. You're tired of men. You're tired of the way they're all the same. You're tired of their self-centeredness, their total cluelessness about your feelings, the way some of them just disappear into thin air when things seemed to be going well. You're tired of having the same conversation again and again, going through the same self-introductory rigmarole—the recitation of your history, the cute stories that define you—only to realize this guy is as much of a bonehead as the last one. But now here you are meeting someone new, and you're supposed to be bright and perky and hopeful? You're supposed to act like you're still twenty-two, even though you're overwhelmed with the *Groundhog Day* feeling that you've been on this exact date 999,999 times before? You're supposed to somehow forget that it didn't work out with those 999,999 other men and ignore the cumulative effect of all those dates: that you're beginning to wonder if you might actually hate men?

I don't blame you for being sick of us. And you know what? I hate to be negative, but we can get sick of you, too: how you string us along when you feel like you need someone to adore you, then shut us down when a richer/cuter/guitar-playing guy comes along; how you can crush our hearts and not feel guilty about it because you're *just being open about your feelings*; how there's always one more thing you want to change about us. Dating women isn't a bowl of cherries all the time either. But back to us: We're not easy. We smell bad. We usually have far too high a regard for ourselves— except when we're feeling low and need someone to tell us how awesome we are over and over again. We think we've finally become comfortable with our emotions, and then someone bares theirs to us, and it's like we're six years old all over again. Multiply that by, say, ten relationships and, again, I can understand why a woman might be filled with a little bit of dread as she waits at a bar in a tight but businessy blouse for me to show up from the gym.

That dread is part of dating. The dread that comes from knowing that most dates aren't going to work out, statistically speaking. But reading the man the riot act won't change that. You may think you're being smart, like you've been around the block a few times, but if you walk in expecting the worst, you're only hurting yourself. You're transmitting negative energy, which doesn't lead to very successful dates and is kind of self-perpetuating. You're actually making what you're afraid of—having a date that goes nowhere—an almost sure thing.

I'm not writing this chapter just because I had a bad date once. I'm writing it because I've met too many women who protected themselves right out of a chance at a decent relationship, or at least a date. I'm writing it because of all the conversations I've had with women who are fed up, *and* the ones I've had with the guys they've gone out with. I'm writing it for my friend Tara, who freaked out on her excellent boyfriend the very first time they had a real argument because she was just *sure* it was going to end with him leaving her. I'm writing it for every *Glamour* reader who's ever lost the forest for the trees, writing in to Jake complaining that "all men suck!" I'm writing it for my friend Mike, who recently sat down to a first-date dinner only to be greeted with what seemed to him like a contractual agreement: "I only want to date guys who are serious about relationships," said his date, "so if you're not, you should collect your things and leave now." I'm writing it for every woman who's afraid to let down her guard with men, to show them her true *inner* power. I'm writing it for women who scold men for being flirtatious or a little rascally, even though these are some of men's best qualities. And finally, I'm writing this chapter to remind all the people I've described above exactly what the forest is that they've lost: It's a mysterious, beautiful, sometimes mazelike wilderness, and exploring it is one of life's most awesome trips.

If you're rolling your eyes right now—if you're saying out loud, "Come on, Jake, a mysterious forest?"—I can understand that. I'm being a little schmaltzy, I realize. But really, what's wrong with that? What's wrong with losing one's cool once in a while and just *going* with life? In fact, isn't a little wild abandon just about the coolest thing there is? What's wrong with giving a cute-but-broke poet a second chance to impress you if he blew it the first time by not picking up the bill? Or kissing new lips just because the guy they're attached to is offering them to you, and they are a fine set of lips? Or realizing that dates in general might be futile in the grand scheme, but you might as well enjoy the ride? Are you with me here? If you are *still* rolling your eyes, well, *maybe you need to be a little bit more French.* I hope I'm sounding impassioned instead of mad. But maybe I am a little angry—frustrated that you're not seizing life a little more.

Why We Should All Be a Little More French

Enjoying life does seem to be one of those things—like making bread, having affairs and aging—that the French know how to do better than we do. I love France, and French women especially. They seem to genuinely love men. Unlike many American women I've known, French women don't feel the need to figure men out or anticipate our every move. They just like being with us. And they don't really give a damn what will happen tomorrow as long as today is enjoyable.

At least this is the impression I've formed based upon a six-day college trip to Paris and my friendship with a particular French woman I've known and admired and crushed on since I was a kid—Beatrice. Beatrice is my childhood neighbor Jenny's mom. *All* men crush on her. She met Jenny's American dad in France in the late sixties, and he asked her to marry him and move with him to New Jersey, where he was from. After some deliberation, she said to her lover, and I quote the family lore: *"Ah, merde, je t'aime! Pourquoi pas?"* (Translation: "Well, shit, I love you! Why not?") Ah, Beatrice, how do I do her justice? She takes chances! She's beautiful without being show-offy. She is an amazing combination of disciplined (she goes for long walks every morning and never overeats) and indulgent (she always orders a dessert to share). She's also at once incredibly feminine (no one her age wears skirts and makeup with more skill and pride than she does) and extremely tough (she will not hesitate to confront anyone, man or woman, when she senses some injustice).

Bottom line, Beatrice has to be the most self-possessed woman I've ever met; she really does believe that no one but she is responsible for making her happy. Her husband, my friend Jenny's dad, worked a lot when we were kids, so I've never really known him, but I do remember him kissing her neck while she washed dishes once or twice. And Jenny has always talked about how in love her parents were—and still are. "Dad worships Mom," says Jenny. "She makes *both* of them feel young, mostly by flirting—with him and with everyone! For her, there's no excuse *not* to flirt your way through life." Now, Jenny doesn't mean "flirt your way through life" as in "come on to every person who crosses your path." That would be icky. What Jenny means is that her mom flirts because it adds a little excitement—*frisson*, as the French say—to what would otherwise be ordinary interactions with ordinary people, including the person she's woken up next to every day for the past forty-something years.

Beatrice flirts with the man who sells her cheese and the man who fills her car with gas. She flirts with her clients (she's an interior decorator). And because flirting isn't always about sex, she even flirts with women, like the policewoman who pulled her over for speeding last year. Beatrice doesn't feel that flirting reduces her to some prefeminist cliché. She does it simply because every encounter she has is a small affirmation that life is full of surprises, and you never know what you might learn from someone just by looking into their eyes.

It's important to note that Beatrice hasn't gone through life wearing rose-colored glasses. She knows men's limitations. And she doesn't shy away from letting the men in her life—her husband, her business partner, even me!—know exactly what she thinks of their shortcomings once in a while. I remember her scolding me for making a too-mature move on my junior high girlfriend and, another time, for not arguing with her when she knew I disagreed about something. She likes to keep men honest, she wants us to expect a bit more from ourselves. But she doesn't begrudge us our maleness. As she once said to Jenny: "Even though men are infuriating sometimes, it doesn't make me love them any less."

I saw Suz—yes, Suz of the very bad date—not long ago. She looked amazing. She was in the full glow of pregnancy. She'd been married a little more than a year and was due to have her baby in five months. And she really shocked me by apologizing only a few minutes into our conversation.

"God," she said, "I'm so sorry for the way our date went." She told me she'd actually been hoping to see me ever since we went out, to let me know that it was her, not me. Apparently our date was the moment she decided she needed to reassess her attitude. "I was just in this mental rut. I thought I had men figured out. I thought I knew what they were after, and that the way to win was to get in their faces immediately. Not the best strategy. I think about all the people I met and acted that way toward, and it's like, 'What a waste!'"

Then she said something that kind of brings to mind all ten of the rules in this book: "I was so concerned with figuring out men and calling them on their shit," said Suz, "that I forgot what *I* wanted, which was to be happy, to have *romance* in my life."

You never know: If things had gone differently that night, maybe Suz would have found her romance with me. But I had disappointed her even before our date started, so we never had a chance. That's such a common pattern: Too often women overlook a man's best attributes because they're too busy focusing on his weakest ones. Blossoms has a saying: "You don't get pissed at Chipotle for not having good fried chicken." Which is to say, you have to realize what each person has to offer, and relish that thing if it's something you want. Enjoy the men you meet for who they are instead of getting pissed about who they're not. He's not neat? But he's creative, and isn't that worth the trade-off? He's not athletic? That's okay, the guy is better with kids than a kindergarten teacher.

I'm not saying you should pretend you don't want a committed relationship if you do. There is absolutely nothing wrong with or weak about wanting to move in with someone and share your life with him. I'm just saying that you're going to have an easier time finding what you're looking for if you stop and remind yourself— one or ten or twenty times a day—that all you can do to control when and how that happens is to be your strongest and most loving self. Take it from me and Suz: Twenty years from now you'll want to be able to look back and feel proud that you lived your dating years with a brave, open heart. This is, after all, a book about power—the power *you* have to find and grow and hold on to the love you're looking for. And it all starts and ends with you claiming the right to love yourself, have fun and feel sexy—instead of waiting around for a guy to make you feel that awesome.

Those of you about to date, or to throw yourself into a new relationship head-on or to recommit yourself to enjoying the one you've been in for years: I salute you. I also ask you to remember that love is grand. It's risky, sure, and filled with moments of frustration and heartbreak and embarrassment—but it's still the most exciting thing around. So if you're dating, remember why you're going on that date in the first place: because what lies before you is the very real possibility that you'll hit the relationship jackpot and make a meaningful connection with someone. That's why your mantra shouldn't be "Dating sucks"; it should be "Dating rocks because *I* rock!" Or, if you're in a relationship, "Love rocks because I rock!"

Love *does* rock. And we should savor it every step of the way. Enjoy the ride. Because the most powerful woman of all is the one who's having *fun*.

How to Use Your Secret Power to Cheat-Proof Your Relationship

A giant part of enjoying the ride is being able to trust your partner, totally and completely. Of course, he's got to *earn* that trust—and you can help him. You can't keep a man intent on straying from doing so, but you *can*, I believe, reduce the odds of infidelity in a generally good relationship. Here's how:

Ask him if he's happy.

First off, you probably *know*, in your heart of hearts, if he's happy. But you still need to talk to him about it, because people tend to cheat if they're not happy. (If you can picture your guy cheating even if he *was* happy, you should find another boyfriend.) The key isn't to make it feel like an inquisition. If he's thinking about cheating, he's going to be feeling guilty and secretive anyway. So start by telling him what you think you want to improve in the relationship, and ask him if he has requests. Tell him what you're looking for in the bedroom, and ask what he wants. If he's willing to talk about this stuff, it's a strong sign that he is committed to your relationship.

Be the other woman yourself.

I know I just said this in Rule #9, but men like mystery, the un-known, the forbidden and the different-from-everyday. If you can occasionally be that mysterious woman yourself—dress differently one night, indulge in a sexual fantasy you've never even discussed before, talk dirty to him in public even though it makes you blush—then all that pent-up sexual desire gets expressed *through* your relationship instead of outside of it.

Give him the freedom to flirt a little.

Your instinct might be to shut down his flirting. This is wrong. A dude who feels he's living under a totalitarian dictatorship is more likely to rebel. If you can find his flirting (as long as it is harmless and not sleazy) attractive, you'll have a lot more fun with him, which will make him want to redirect his energy back to you.

Make sure *you're* sexually satisfied.

Conventional wisdom would say you should make sure *he's* sexually satisfied so he won't have excess horniness to spread around. And sure, that's part of it. But pay attention to your own desires and feelings. Because you want to have an empowered, happy relationship, right? But also because a woman who's in touch with her own sexuality is far more satisfying to be with, in and out of bed—which makes cheating less likely.

Epilogue

....

A Letter to the Women of America:
Four Things I Really, Truly Hope You Will Know About
Men—and Yourself—by the Time You Close This Book

....

Dear Jess:

Sorry to call you Jessica. Just figured there might be at least a couple of you out there. But let's talk seriously for a moment. In a way, I feel like a big brother to you. Like a big brother who wants you to have everything you want in life: respect, power, and the heart of a guy who gets, I mean, *really gets* how lucky he is to be loved by you. I might even lock you in your room for a second while I chase your "friend with benefits" off the property. You deserve better than that! I guess I just feel protective.

Since I've just spent an entire book telling you how to know what you want, and get it, with men, I want to make sure you were listening. So I'm going to leave you with a cheat sheet. Here are four things never to forget about yourself, and your relationships:

······································· **LESSON 1** ·······································

You are an extraordinary, singular person.

··

You know what made me realize this about you, Jessica, and about all the women out there who may not be named Jessica? My daughter. In a strange way, I see almost every person I meet now the way a father (or at least that really protective big brother) would. It's made me about 1,000 percent more compassionate, and so much more awake to the thousand ways people can be exceptional. And just like my daughter, I want you to feel like the most worthy, intelligent, beautiful woman in any room you enter—because to the right people, you will be. It seems simplistic to say this, but if you know how sexy you are, I will bet my Mets cap that one day the right guy will know it too. Feeling completely worthy of enormous helpings of total love will help you *find that love.*

······································· **LESSON 2** ·······································

This is going to be fun.

··

Listen, you've read the last chapter in this book. This is dating, it's not a root canal. Go in with a sense of adventure, not a desire for Novocain. Bring your sense of discovery, your compassion for all humankind. Be playful—that's what hitting on the wingman is all about. Be yourself—cheer for the Mets if you love them, don't if you don't. But know that it isn't always going to be easy. If you think you're not going to feel a little bit nervous, to doubt your feelings once in a while, to feel a little insecure—well, you're not allowing yourself to be a human being! The only thing better than falling in love at first sight is falling in love a little bit at a time. And if it feels a little scary, remember: So do roller coasters! And they're *awesome*.

LESSON 3

Men can be immature. Even the good ones.

Before my daughter was born two and a half years ago, I always told myself I wasn't going to be that clichéd dad. You know the one: the guy who answers the door with a shotgun when his daughter's prom date arrives; the dad who makes jokes about sending his daughter to a convent until she's thirty. But when I imagine my little girl getting ready for her first date—the hope in her heart—I can understand why I might need a twelve-gauge. Because I was a very young man once, too. And if I'm totally honest, I wouldn't want *any* young woman to date someone who's anything like me back then: the me I was before I finally got the courage to take a flying leap and commit to the woman I married. But I also understand that it's inevitable that the right guy for you—or, yes, even my daughter—will have a flawed past, that he'll make his share of relationship mistakes. That's okay, as long as he's come through on the other side with a bigger heart and with his head (finally) screwed on straight. So don't rule out the immature guy, the guy whose manners aren't impeccable, or even the guy who needs to be led gently to the whole commitment idea.

········· **LESSON 4** ·········

Despite all that, you might get hurt.

In fact, you *will*. If you're doing the dating thing right, at some point you're going to get your feelings in a twist, your pride wounded or even your heart broken. It's inevitable, because if you're not taking risks, you're not on that roller coaster. And while my instinct as big brother Jake is to protect you from that, I would be doing you a disservice if I did. To be protected is not to live.

But given all that—given that relationships are scary and that most men are a little immature—it usually works out. Look around. The hopeful signs—excellent relationships, wonderful marriages, sex lives that stay sexy for decades and decades—are everywhere. So don't get beleaguered. I never want you to stop expecting real, transcendent love. It's out there, and I found it; you can, and you will, too.

That's my last lesson: You are going to find something beautiful. You never know when it's going to happen. And while I know you'll be let down any time you're looking for that beautiful thing and don't find it, I want you to stay disappointed for only seven minutes. Or maybe two days. Because it's a waste of time. Instead, spend your time having fun, dating men and finding love. Don't worry about whatever timelines your bouquet-tossing girlfriends are on. Soon enough you'll find what you're looking for and you'll wish you had let go and enjoyed yourself more along the way. What I'm about to say is the hokiest thing I've ever said (which follows the four or five other hokiest things I've ever said, previously, in this letter), but here it is: Every moment is joy. And my hope for you is that you feel the joy in every moment.

Now get out there and make me proud,

JAKE

Acknowledgments

If there's one thing I learned from writing the Jake column, it's that you're only as good as the women in your life. They inspire you, reject you, accept you, lecture you, make you take your vitamins and all in all teach you to be a better man. Go figure that almost everyone I have to thank is a woman: my *Glamour* editors Jill Herzig and Genevieve Field, who made me dig deep and become a worthy Jake; Orange Blossoms, for showing me your secret powers; L'il Blossoms, for promising not to use yours on other men for several decades at least; Mom, for showing me how to think independently and making me really want to be only with women who do too; and the friends, coworkers, ex-girlfriends, ex-flings and ex-almost-flings whose names are changed in these pages. If you recognize yourself (and therefore me, hi!), please don't tell anyone, OK? And, thank you, Bud Palmer, and all fifty-six years' worth of Jakes, for your openness and honesty.

I'm also grateful for everyone at *Glamour* and Hyperion who made this book possible: Cindi Leive, Lauren Brody, Susan Goodall, Ellen Archer, Elisabeth Dyssegaard, Christine Pride, Geraldine Hessler, Sarah Viñas, Wendy Naugle, Devin Tomb, Carla Murphy, Jessica Duncan, Alison Goldman, Vanessa Weiman, Leslie Yudell, Stacy Cousino, Samantha Rosenthal, Susie Draper, and Jen Weinberg.

And most important, thanks to the 12 million women who helped me so much: the readers of *Glamour*, who trusted me with their questions and their hearts, and made me man up in the process.